NAVAL POSTGRADUATE SCHOOL
Monterey, California

THESIS

DESIGN OF RELATIONAL DATABASE BENCHMARKS

by

Vincent Courtney Stone

June 1983

Thesis Advisor: David K. Hsiao

Approved for public release; distribution unlimited

SECURITY CLASSIFICATION OF THIS PAGE (When Data Entered)

REPORT DOCUMENTATION PAGE		READ INSTRUCTIONS BEFORE COMPLETING FORM
1. REPORT NUMBER	2. GOVT ACCESSION NO.	3. RECIPIENT'S CATALOG NUMBER
4. TITLE (and Subtitle) Design of Relational Database Benchmarks		5. TYPE OF REPORT & PERIOD COVERED Master's Thesis June, 1983
		6. PERFORMING ORG. REPORT NUMBER
7. AUTHOR(s) Vincent Courtney Stone		8. CONTRACT OR GRANT NUMBER(s)
9. PERFORMING ORGANIZATION NAME AND ADDRESS Naval Postgraduate School Monterey, California 93940		10. PROGRAM ELEMENT, PROJECT, TASK AREA & WORK UNIT NUMBERS
11. CONTROLLING OFFICE NAME AND ADDRESS Naval Postgraduate School Monterey, California 93940		12. REPORT DATE June 1983
		13. NUMBER OF PAGES 112
14. MONITORING AGENCY NAME & ADDRESS(if different from Controlling Office)		15. SECURITY CLASS. (of this report) UNCLASSIFIED
		15a. DECLASSIFICATION/DOWNGRADING SCHEDULE

16. DISTRIBUTION STATEMENT (of this Report)

Approved for public release; distribution unlimited

17. DISTRIBUTION STATEMENT (of the abstract entered in Block 20, if different from Report)

18. SUPPLEMENTARY NOTES

19. KEY WORDS (Continue on reverse side if necessary and identify by block number)

benchmarking, database machines

20. ABSTRACT (Continue on reverse side if necessary and identify by block number)

Performance measurements of a database machine reflect not only the processing power of the machine, but also the size and structure of the database. It is therefore useful to construct databases for performance measurements of database machines. Furthermore, it is useful to utilize synthetic data, such that the volume of the reply can be predicted for a given query and the structure and attributes of the database can be varied (Continued)

DD FORM 1473 EDITION OF 1 NOV 65 IS OBSOLETE
1 JAN 73
S/N 0102-LF-014-6601

1

SECURITY CLASSIFICATION OF THIS PAGE (When Data Entered)

ABSTRACT (Continued)   Block # 20

for intended test queries. Conducting measurement studies using
a synthetic database contributes to the generality of the results
when different test queries are employed. A parameterized program
is described herein which can be used to generate various relations for a synthetic database. The experiences in constructing
and using the database generator are described. It is suggested
that given sufficient information on real-world databases the
generator may be useful for modeling them as well as for creating
databases for benchmark tests.

Design of

Relational Database Benchmarks

by

Vincent Courtney Stone
Lieutenant Commander, United States Navy
B.S., United States Naval Academy, 1974

Submitted in partial fulfillment of the
requirements for the degree of

MASTER OF SCIENCE IN COMPUTER SCIENCE

from the

NAVAL POSTGRADUATE SCHOOL
June, 1983

ABSTRACT

Performance measurements of a database machine reflect
not only the processing power of the machine, but also the
size and structure of the database.   It is therefore useful
to construct databases for performance measurements of database machines.   Furthermore, it is useful   to utilize
synthetic data,   such   that the volume of the reply can   be
predicted for a given query and the structure and attributes
of   the   database can be varied for intended   test   queries.
Conducting   measurement studies using a   synthetic   database
contributes   to the generality of the results when different
test queries are employed.   A parameterized program is   described   herein   which   can   be   used   to   generate   various
relations for a synthetic database.   The experiences in constructing and using the database generator are described   It
is suggested that given sufficient information on real-world
databases   the generator may be useful for modeling them   as
well as for creating databases for benchmark tests.

TABLE OF CONTENTS

4

5

List of Figures

LIST OF TABLES

8

ACKNOWLEDGEMENTS

I would like to ackowledge the help and support of the following people in the preparation of this thesis: Doris Mleczko and the staff of the Data Processing Support Center, West, Point Magu, California, CDR T. M. Pigoski, USN, Naval e Security Group Headquarters, Paula R. Strawser, my second reader and overseer and Dr. David K. Hsaio, my advisor.

I would also like to note that the work performed in support of this thesis has been performed in concert with the thesis work of LCDR Curtis J. Ryder, USN, LT Robert A. Bogianowicz, and LT Michael D. Crocker.

I. BENCHMARKS FOR DATABASE MACHINES

A. PERFORMANCE MEASUREMENTS

In comparing database management systems (DBMSs) an
important factor is their performance. One way to compare
DBMSs is to run specific applications under a variety of
systems. Each system can be 'fine-tuned' to give the best
result. An evaluation based on such a method is costly and
time-consuming. Often such a method may be infeasible. In
many cases, a database for the specific applications may
not even exist. As a second method, an evaluation could be
made on the basis of performance measurements of existing
databases. This method is less costly and less time-consuming. However, the following questions arise. Is the
existing database sufficient to support intended applications? Are the applications good for condu ting relative
performance evaluation of different DBMSs?

It is impractical to perform such direct comparison of
DBMSs. Adapting an application to several systems for evaluation purposes is not practical. Evaluation based on
existing databases is subject to interpretation error. The
increasing number of DBMSs makes it imperative that some
method is to be devised to do comparative performance
measurements.

10

B. BENCHMARKING

The concept of a standard for measuring performance is not new. The standard is usually known as a benchmark, after the markers used by surveyors in establishing a common reference point for their measurements. For example, Mount Diablo (a mountain east of San Francisco) is used as the reference point in surveying much of Northern California due to its long-range visibility. A method for measuring similar items in reference to a standard is called benchmarking.

Precedents for benchmarking exist in measuring the performance of computer systems. The Gibson-Mix method measures the execution time of a specific set of application programs for benchmarking computer systems. The expected performance of a system could be computed by characterizing the expected workload as a mix of jobs from the standard set.

It is proposed that a set of application programs can be devised to measure the performance of DBMSs. Using these benchmark measurements, it will be possible to compare the performance of various DBMSs. The measurements can be analyzed to suggest strengths and weaknesses of the DBMSs.

C. QUANTITIES TO BE MEASURED

The generally accepted performance index for a DBMS is the response time. Defining the response time as the

11

primary performance index is the scope of this research. However, the response time is based on several factors. Among these factors are the time to process the query, the time to access the data, the time to process data, and the time to return the data. For a DBMS running on a mainframe computer, the effects of other workload on the response time must also be considered.

A measurement of the response time is more significant when measurements of its components are provided. Some simplifying assumptions may be made. The first such assumption is that the rate of accessing data in the database is constant. The second is that the rate of returning processed data is constant. However, the time involved in the processing of queries and the time involved in the processing of data may vary greatly among database operations. It order to record the variance of time among the operations, tests must be devised which will indicate these components for all supported operations.

This thesis focuses on measurements of the response time. A development of a system to measure components of the response time is discussed. The system involves the generation of a synthetic database. The system also measures the benchmarked machine in using that database.

II.   BENCHMARKING RELATIONAL DATABASE MACHINES

A.   THE BENCHMARKING ENVIRONMENT

The research done in support of this thesis has been performed in a complex environment. The complexity involves multiple machines and multiple operating systems.

A Relation Generator (RG) of synthetic relations has been developed using Pascal (i.e., IBM's Pascal/VS) in a multiuser environment (VM/CMS running on IBM 3033). RG is used in a batch environment (MVS) on the same machine. The relations are generated in EBCDIC-character form. They are transported to a UNIVAC 1100 via tape. The EBCDIC files are then loaded onto the host (i.e., the UNIVAC computer) and translated by the host into ASCII files. These ASCII files are finally loaded into a backend database machine (i.e., Britton Lee's IDM 500).

The backend machine and interface software for the 1100 series computers are marketed by the Amperif Corporation of Chatsworth, California, as the RDM 1100. Additional measurements can be made by bypassing the part of the query processor that provides terminal support. This is accomplished by communicating directly with the query processor via compiled language statements (i.e., COBOL). This does not completely bypass the query processor, because the query language is interpreted and cannot be precompiled. However,

the results show that query processing does not represent a significant portion of the response time if the host workload is light. The terminal handler represents also a small portion of the response time. Therefore, the only advantage to the use of compiled programs is the option of running the process as a background job.

B. THE ARCHITECTURE OF THE SYSTEM

The architecture of the system encompasses two major areas. The first of these areas is the internal architecture of the IDM 500. The second area is the host system software, i.e., the user interface which runs on the host.

1. The Basic Machine Architecture and Various Configurations

The IDM 500 is made up of several modules connected to a common high-speed bus (See Figure 1). The database processor is a 6-mhz, Zilog Z-8000 series microprocessor which performs the DBMS functions. The coding for the microprocessor is written largely in the C programming language, along with some assembly language routines. It comprises about 330 k-bytes of machine code. An optional module, the database accelerator improves the system performance by implementing in high-speed, special-purpose hardware some of the DBMS functions normally performed by the database processor.

14

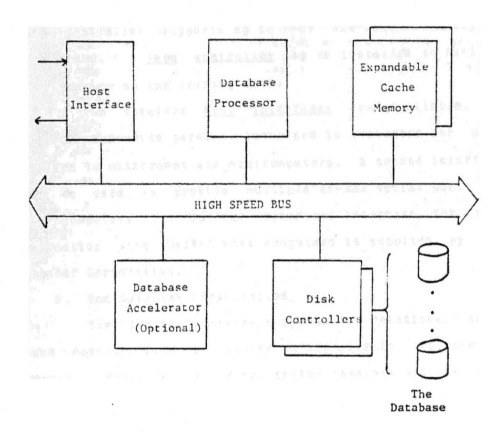

HIGH SPEED BUS

The Database

Figure 1 - The IDM Bus Architecture

15

The cache memory is composed of 64k-bit dynamic RAM chips. The basic configuration (at the beginning of the tests) included one-half megabyte of memory. Up to six megabytes of memory can be supported. During the testing period, configurations of one and two megabytes have also been used.

One to four disk controllers may be installed. Each controller supports up to four six-hundred-megabyte, hard disks. A tape controller may be installed to facilitate backing up and loading data.

Two standard host interfaces are available. A IEEE-488 byte-wide parallel interface is available for connection to mainframes and minicomputers. A second interface can be used to provide multiple RS-232 serial ports to microcomputers. A special byte/word interface for communication with UNIVAC host computers is supplied by the Amperif Corporation.

2. The Database Organization

The IDM 500 software supports the relational database model. Data is stored on the disk in two logical levels. These levels are the system database and the user databases. At the top level, the system database contains five system tables and thirteen database tables. The system tables contain information on hardware configuration, databases and current usage. The thirteen database tables comprise the data dictionary. They are used to

16

store information about relations, attributes, users, and security. A list of the system tables and the database tables is given in Appendix A.

Although access to the system database is required for the creation of a user database, an existing user database can be accessed directly, i.e., without going through the system database. Each user database has both database tables and user tables. The database tables are stored within the user database and may be accessed in the same manner as user tables.

The basic unit of disk access is a 2k-byte block. When a database is created, a space allocation in blocks may be requested. This allocation may be increased if necessary. Both system tables and database tables are used by the system to compute physical addresses.

3. The User Interface

The user interface is accessed by invoking an process on the host. This process is an interactive query processor. The query processor parses the user's queries written in the Relational Query Language (RQL). RQL is Amperif's implementation of Britton-Lee's Intelligent Query Language (IQL). Alternatively, queries may be submitted to the query processor from a compiled COBOL or FORTRAN program. Submitting a compiled program as a batch job, the user may bypass the query processor's terminal handler.

However, the batch job still depends on the query processor for parsing of the query.

The Relational Query Language (RQL) provides operations and facilities similar to those available on relational DBMSs currently running on mainframe computers and larger minicomputers. RQL also allows queries to be pre-parsed and stored within a database. These stored commands limit the time required in the host for parsing and reduce the time required in the backend for the database-table lookup. Additional information on RQL may be found in [1, 2 and 3].

Communication with the IDM is via a system process, RDMIO. RDMIO supervises communications between user processes running on the host and the hardware interface to the IDM (See Figure 2). Up to ten users may access the RDM simultaneously from a single UNIVAC host.

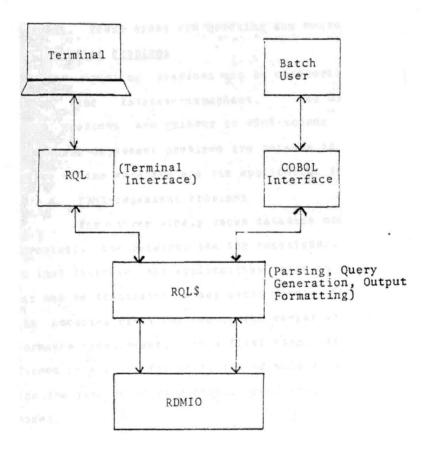

Figure 2 - The IDM/User Interface

19

III. THE BENCHMARKING APPROACH

A. A MULTI-DIMENSIONAL PROBLEM

Creating a benchmarking system poses a problem with several dimensions. The problem can be broken down into two major areas. These areas are modeling and measurement.

1. Modeling Problems

The modeling problems can be categorized as DBMS-dependent and database-dependent. The DBMS-dependent modeling problems are related to DBMS schema and syntax. The database-dependent problems are related to the characteristics of the database and the application to be modeled.

a. DBMS-dependent Problems

The three widely known database models are the hierarchical, the network, and the relational. It has been shown that databases and applications based on one of these models can be translated to any other model. However, there is no accepted basis for meaningful comparisons of their performance measurement. As a first step, tests have been performed in support for establishing such a basis for DBMSs having the same underlying model, specifically the relational model.

b. Database-dependent Problems

The database-dependent problems are representative of existing databases and the applications which are

used on them. Existing databases vary in the complexity and in the efficiency in which they have been implemented. These varieties are partly due to the physical data that are represented in the database and partly due to the programmers' abilities to construct the database. Additionally, the applications which use these databases also model the physical data represented as well as the information required of the database. Thus, both existing databases and applications must be modeled. The key to an effective and general model is creating one which represents common characteristics. The characteristics of databases and applications must be carefully studied prior to the design of a general and effective model. The contrasting nature of existing databases and their applications present an extremely complex modeling problem.

2. Measurement Problems

DBMS benchmark measurements, as a standard, may also represent a comparison of DBMS performance. This standard may be either absolute or relative. Absolute measurements assume a fixed standard. Relative measurements may provide rankings within a group of DBMSs. The measurement of the response time for relative ranking is our goal.

Experiments must be constructed carefully and the environment must be controlled to provide useable, accurate measurements. For example, in performing research for this

21

thesis it has been noticed that the load on the host can significantly affect the response time as seen by the user. Similarly, the response time is heavily affected by the time required to return the data to the user at the screen. These effects must be minimized in order to obtain measurements which more accurately reflect the performance of the backend database machine. Resolution of measurement problems is discussed in Section V.B.

B. RESOLVING THE MODELING PROBLEMS

Although the modeling problems cannot be eliminated, steps can be taken to minimize the errors introduced by the modeling process.

1. DBMS-dependent Problems

Two assumptions can be made to minimize the DBMS-dependent modeling errors. These assumptions concern the format of the data and the operations used to access the data.

The first assumption is that all relations are stored in third normal form (3NF). The use of 3NF minimizes the possibility of inconsistent data. While real databases do not use 3NF, this fact doesn't discourage our assumption. The benchmark is designed to provide a measurement of DBMSs' performance. It is not intended to take into consideration

the abilities of those persons who will design the databases (although ease of use may be a consideration in some instances), for they may not understand the theory of 3NF.

The second assumption to be made is that the query languages used by the DBMSs are logically equivalent. Although differences in syntax do exist, they generally do not affect the breadth of available operations. Therefore, a common set of queries can be implemented in the DBMSs' individual syntaxes and provide the identical logical result. Any variations to this should be noted with benchmark results. The basic set of experiments include selections, projections, joins, updates, insertions and deletions. Additionally experiments should be performed which test the performance of any peculiar or powerful operations which a DBMS may have in addition to the standard set.

2. Database-dependent Problems

The elimination of database-dependent modeling problems involves two fundamental areas. The first of these areas is the generation of a synthetic database. The generation of such a database allows the use of data which is generally representative of existin databases, but not specifically representative of any one. The design of the synthetic database's characteristics should be broad. This ensures that it can be adapted to realistically measure the performance of a database with its own characteristics. These characteristics include the sizes of the relations (in

23

the number of tuples and tuple length) in the database and
the length of a tuple relative to block size of the storage
medium.

The second area involving database dependency
involves the applications running on the database. A synthetic workload is required for the same reasons as for the
synthetic database. The design of the synthetic workload
should be broad enough to provide enough results to be able
to fully simulate different applications. The workload is
designed with two major considerations. The first consideration is support of the basic relational operations
discussed previously. An additional consideration takes
into account the varying access patterns of existing databases. For example, a given application may repeatedly
retrieve only one tuple at a time. Another will retrieve
many in one operation. An important characteristic is the
locality of the data retrieved by operations. This characteristic may produce different levels of performance with
different indexing methods.

C. THE SYNTHESIZED DATABASE AND WORKLOAD

1. The Use of Synthesized Data

In determining a set of benchmark measurements, it
is necessary to obtain the set which can be used on a wide
range of DBMSs. It is also important that this set does not
favor any DBMS or class of DBMSs.

24

Two approaches could have been taken in obtaining measurements. One approach would be to perform tests on existing databases. The other approach is to do measurements on a synthetic database. The latter allows the greatest flexibility in performing operations on the database. This is because the schema of a real database might not provide a suitable structure for performing a test of some operations. The schema of a synthetic database, on the other hand minimizes any bias resulting from designing the tests around a particular database.

The research for this thesis is performed in conjunction with evaluation of relational database machines. However, the installation has no relational databases. Therefore, any tests on the DBMS would have to be performed on either a synthetic database or a database converted from another model. Since the use of synthetic databases supports a more general approach in benchmarking, the choice has been made to generate such databases for benchmarking tests.

2. Types of Synthesized Data

Synthesized data should have one major characteristic. The types of data should be broad enough to test the supported DBMS operations of different types of fields (i.e., values). For example, in the research performed for this thesis, the first two attribute values of each relation

have the same numeric value. However, the first attribute value is stored as an integer and the second as a character string. One set of tests selects tuples based on the integer values; a second set of tests selects the same tuples based on character values. Response times may be affected by the processing differences related to the data types. Additional differences may result from the time required to format the data for output.

3. General Schema of Synthesized Data Used

The synthesized data used for this thesis has four sets of relations. Each set has several relations with different numbers of tuples. Each relation in a set has the same attributes. The attributes are similar among the four sets, differing only in number and length in order to provide a range of tuple lengths. Table 1 shows the range of tuple characteristics.

The relations are stored in several databases. Two databases are used for testing single-relation operations. The first database contains all of the relations used in single relation testing. The second database contains relations whose tuples are of 100 bytes and 200 bytes. This database uses compressed fields for strings (i.e., trailing blanks are dropped) . Several databases are used to provide relations for testing join operations. For testing, it is desirable to spread the join operations over the two disks in the system. A full implementation of this desirable

26

Table 1. The Relation Characteristics

Tuple Lengths   : 100, 200, 1000, 2000 Bytes

Relation Logical Sizes   : 500, 1000, 2500, 5000, 10000 Tuples

Relation Physical Sizes   : 50 kilobytes to 20 megabytes

Attributes   : 14 (for 100 byte tuples), 24 (for
                             other tuple lengths)

Attribute Types   : Sequential Integer, Random Integer,
                             Collated Alphanumeric, Blocks Sets

database placement is not possible, because the storage
allocation algoritnms prevent us from controlling over the
storage location of specific relations.

IV. GENERATING SYNTHESIZED DATA

A. A PARAMETERIZED RELATION GENERATOR

The Relation Generator (RG) is a parameterized program for generating relations for a database. RG prompts the user concerning the characteristics of a relation. First the user is instructed to enter the relation name and size (i.e., the number of tuples). Then, the program requests data about each attribute. The data equested includes attribute name, value type (i.e., integer, string, etc.) and distribution of the attribute values. The relations generated are stored in ASCII files to simplify transfer between systems.

1. Capabilities

RG contains routines to generate sequential numbers, random numbers (either uniquely or nonuniquely), and character strings in collated order (See Appendix B). The user may also specify a file which contains a set of values for an attribute to be used in generating attribute values. This set is called a 'value-set' and the file is called a value-set file. It is produced by the utility program, Value-set Generator (described below). The actual range of values from the file to be used for an attribute is called the attribute's domain. The user specifies the number of values from the value-set to be included in the attribute's

domain. It is not necessary that the domain contain all the values in the value-set. RG requires the user to define the distribution of the attribute values. The distribution is either in discrete blocks or random or both. A discrete distribution in which the attribute values are randomly distributed may be created by sorting a relation containing discrete blocks on a random number attribute.

2. The Development

a. The Development Environment

RG is written in IBM Pascal/VS, running under the VM/CMS operating system. VM/CMS is an interactive, multiuser operating system. Beacause of operating system limitations, RG has been converted to a MVS (batch) process. Standard Pascal syntax has been utilized as much as possible. Pascal/VS extensions to the language have been used. Additionally, some of the file descriptor information is specific to the operating systems.

b. The Development Process

The first step in the development of the system is the drafting of a modular framework. Persons are then assigned to develop the different modules of the program. The different modules include the main program, the main generator module and the individual value-type generator modules. The individual modules produce specific types of values for the attributes.

30

The system has been developed using modern software engineering techniques. The different modules have been debugged separately. Program harnesses, which contain no logic except to invoke a procedure, have been used to test procedures and subprocedures. Module stubs, which simulate the actions usually performed by procedures, have been used in place of the procedures to test the main program and the main generator module. Once debugged, the modules have been integrated with the main program.

The responsibility for generating relations has been assigned to one person. Additional development of the system involved several items in addition to debugging. A utility to generate value-set files has also been created. Thus, the other members of the team have been freed to work on other phases of the project.

c. Design Problems

Two major problems have been encountered in the preparation of RG. The first problem is the size of the relations to be generated. In the original RG design, all of the linked lists of attribute values reside in the primary memory simultaneously. The size of the largest relation that has been generated is twenty megabytes. This requires twenty megabytes of the virtual memory space just to store the contents of the lists. Additional space would be required for the program and the overhead associated with linked lists (i.e., pointers to memory locations). This

31

exceeds the virtual memory space available to a single user under VM/CMS.

This problem has been partially solved by accessing sequential files as a substitute for the linked lists. Therefore only one list of attribute values at a time is stored in the primary memory. However, a linked list of some of the longer attributes generated requires over two megabytes of memory just for the data, without considering the space required for pointers.

The second problem concerns the transportation of the files of generated relations to another system. Under the VM/CMS system at the Naval Postgraduate School, each user is allowed a limited amount of file space. This amount is much too small to hold most of the relations generated. Additional space is available on a temporary (i.e., one-day) basis. Also important is the fact that while VM/CMS files can be offloaded to tape, they are stored on tape in a non-standard format. There is no utility program to transfer VM/CMS files to tape in standard format. There is also no utility program to exchange files between the tapes of VM/CMS format and the tapes of MVS format.

It is apparent that VM/CMS is not the ideal environment in which to run the system. Therefore, it has been necessary to convert the system to run in the MVS environment. The MVS system writes tapes in the standard

32

format. It also allows the user to have a much larger
virtual memory space. In retrospect, it makes sense to
develop the system in an interactive system (i.e., VM/CMS).
Fast turnaround contributes to faster program development,
and the interactive environment makes debugging easier.

B. A MATRIX OF RELATIONS

The relations generated by RG are designed to support
experiments over a range of relation sizes and characteristics. These sizes and characteristics are selected to allow
maximum flexibility in pursuing experiments with a minimal
number of relations in the test database. The parameters
discussed below are those of the relations produced in support of the benchmarking.

1. Standard Templates

All of the relations are characterized by the same
general template. This template is shown in Table 2. Four
specific templates are derived from the general one. These
templates correspond to the four tuple lengths used for
testing (i.e., 100 bytes, 200 bytes, 1000 bytes and 2000
bytes). Each template is used to generate the relations of
various sizes (500 - 10,000 tuples). Thus most of the tests
can be run on many relations by changing only the relation
name (or the values of the range variable) in the queries.

33

Table 2. General Relation Template

Key   - a sequential number to be stored as an in-
                       teger field

Mirror   - a sequential number (same as key) to be
                       stored as a character string

Random   - a random number to be stored as an integer
                       field

                  *
Random Unique   - a unique random number to be stored as an
                       integer field

Collated   - a character string to be stored in alphabetic or-
                       der

          *
Letter   - a random alphabetical letter

        #
Sets   - blocks of values from value-set files.

    * not used in some templates

    # multiple attributes depending on the tuple length

34

2. Flexibility

The relations are designed to provide flexibility in testing. Ideally the tests to be performed are known before designing the relations. However, the results from some of the tests may suggest a need for additional tests which have not been previously considered. Accordingly, the relations are designed to allow the design of additional tests without generating more relations.

C. THE GENERATING PROCEDURE

The generating procedure consists of three phases. The first phase consists of designing experiments and the relations to be used in those experiments. After the relations have been designed, they must be created and transported to the testing environment.

Generating relations is a simple process. First VG, is used to generate any necessary value-set files. Then, RG is used to generate relations. RG has been expanded to produce a description file. This file contains the attribute names and characteristics of the attribute values in the relation. The description lists both the format of the generated file and the format of the relation as it is to be stored in the database.

1. The Generator System

The generator system consists of two major programs, the Relation Generator (RG) and the Value-set Generator

(V3). Other programs and debugging aids may be necessary, depending on the environment(s) in which the system is implemented.

a. The Relation Generator (RG)

RG creates a relation file based on input from the user. It consists of four types of modules: the main program, the main generator module, the individual generator modules, and the collating module.

The Main Module - The main RG module contains very simple logic. RG prompts the user for the characteristics of the relation being generated. First, the name and size (in tuples) of the relation is requested. Then, the user is asked to determine the characteristics of the first attribute. The attribute characteristics are collected in an attribute record (See Table 3). After the module obtains the necessary attribute characteristics, it invokes the main generator module.

The main generator module, as explained in the next section produces linked lists of attribute values and returns to the main RG module. RG then invokes the collate module which is detailed in the sequel. The collate module produces tuples by concatenating sets of attribute values. After the relation has been generated, the user is given the option of generating another relation or ending the process.

The Main Generator Module - The main generator module is invoked to produce each set of attribute values.

36

Table. 3 <u>The Schema of an Attribute Record</u>

Attribute Name	— assigned attribute name
Attribute Type	— data type of attribute values
String Length	— used for string types
Lower Bound	— first sequential integer and lower bound for random integers
Upper Bound	— upper bound on random integers
Generate Mode	— data-type distribution
Value Set Name	— value-set file name
Relative Proportions	— discrete distribution specification
Seed	— random integers

The characteristics of an attribute are passed to the module in an attribute record. Using this record, the main module invokes one of several individual generator modules, depending on the characteristics of the attribute. The individual generator module produces a linked list of attribute values with the desired type and distribution, and returns the list to the main generator module. The main generator module opens a sequential file, writes the attribute values into the file, closes the file, and returns to the main RG module. There are therefore several such files, known as attribute files.

Collate Module - The collate module acts as a collator. It physically concatenates strings of attribute values to form a tuple. It is invoked to assimilate all the attribute values in the attribute files into a file of the relation. Information describing the attributes is passed to the collator as an array of attribute records. The collator first opens the relation file, and all the attribute files. The relation is generated a tuple at a time. One attribute value from each file is read. The values are concatenated to produce a tuple. The tuple is then written to the relation file. The collator repeats this process until all the tuples have been produced.

b. The Value-set Generator (VG)

The Value-set Generator (VG) is a simple utility for setting up value-set files for RG. VG asks for the name

and size (i.e., the number of values) of the value-set file to be created. The values are entered individually and stored as strings in a random-access file for use by RG.

2. The Conversion Problem

Converting the program to run in the batch environment involves several tasks. These are the conversion of interactive programs to batch programs, the submission of jobs to the batch system, and development of the additional statements required to use of the batch file system. Although the programs had already been debugged in the VM/CMS environment, extensive debugging has been necessary after conversion to MVS.

Conversion of programs from VM/CMS to MVS is not a simple process. A virtual card deck is created in a VM/CMS file which contains the source deck, the input data and the file data required by the MVS system. This file is submitted to the batch queue. The input for RG (i.e., the user's replies) are in the card deck with the program.

Although it is not necessary, the source code which generated the instructions to the user for the input has been removed for the MVS versions. The VM/CMS version has been modified to create a file which contains the user's responses to the program's prompts.

Differences between the batch and interactive systems caused the difficulty in program conversion. The

batch system, MVS, requires much more in the way of file parameter specifications, and is much less forgiving when error conditions exist. There are some error conditions which the user can not foresee. For example, the system may initially allocate space for a relation file on a volume which does not have enough free space to cover secondary allocations. When this happens the program is aborted. However, it is not possible for the user to specify a particular disk (i.e., one with sufficient space) for file storage. For the two largest relation files (fifteen and twenty megabytes), it has been necessary to write each of the relations into two separate files on the batch system. The two files were then combined when they loaded into the database.

    3.   Transporting the Relations to the Testbed

        a. Transporting the Data to the Host

           The transportation of the relations to the host is a two-step process. The first step is the transfer of the relation files from the MVS secondary storage to tape. A system utility is used to accomplish this. The tapes are then transported to the host, the UNIVAC 1100, and a similar utility program is used to load data into the host secondary storage. The host utility program translates the EBCDIC tape files into ASCII disk files.

        b. Loading Data Into the Backend

           The relations are loaded into the backend using

40

a vendor-supplied utility called a translator. This utility
prompts the user for information about the source file, the
target database, and the target relation

The translator utility may be run interactively
or with file input. The database into which the relation is
to be loaded must already exist.   The relation into which
data is loaded may or may not exist.   Database name, host
file name, and relation name must be supplied. Additionally, for each attribute the attribute name, length of source
(in ASCII characters), and type of value to be stored in the
database must be supplied.

V. GENERATING TEST PROGRAMS

A. THE TEST PLAN

The general test plan calls for several different types of experiments. Among these are experiments involving only one relation (i.e., selections and projections) and experiments involving more than one database (i.e., joins).

1. Experiments Involving a Single Relation

The selection and projection experiments are designed to measure the system's performance in retrieving data from a single relation. The response times measured are the sum of four variables: the time to process a query, the time to access the data, the time to process the data, and the time to return the data. The time to process the query is defined as the time to parse the query. By carefully constructing sets of experiments, these variables can be estimated.

Since the time to process a query is so small, it may be ignored or combined with overhead for most experiments. For experiments where it is significant, the query-proccessing time is minimized to prevent it from dominating the time measurement, resulting in a loss of precision. The RDM 1100 allows the parse tree of a query to be stored in the database. This capability allows the replacement of the processing time, which is dependent on

the host, with the data access time, which is dependent only on the backend. The additional data access time is the time to access the command in storage. This is the same for all stored commands.

The largest variables are the easiest to measure with precision. Therefore, they are measured first and then eliminated to measure the smaller variables.

The largest variables are likely to be those representing the time to access, process and return data. These can be measured with simple retrieve commands. A time measurement of a retrieve which returns all the attribute values of the tuples in a relation includes the times of all of the four variables. However, a time measurement using an aggregate function (e.g., count, which returns a single count of the tuples meeting the qualifications of the query) eliminates the time to return the data. Thus this function can be used effectively to measure the time to access and process the data (tuples), i.e., two of the four variables.

Further, an assumption is made that for simple commands the processor can process data at a rate which is faster than the rate that data can be brought into the memory for processing. This allows the processing time to be ignored. Therefore, the measurements reduce to a measure of the access time.

43

Having quantified the larger variables, the time to process data may be investigated. It has been assumed that the processing time is not significant for simple commands. However, if the commands are made more complex, then the processing time is expected to increase. With a sufficiently complex command which involves a small data-access time, the processing time may become significant. Therefore, experiments are conducted which minimize data access but vary in complexity. It is of interest to determine when or if the processing time becomes measureable and significant.

It is expected that projections operations will increase the processing time. Therefore, several tests are appropriate for testing projections. The first set of tests measure the effect of projections on the processing time. The second set checks to see if the processing time is affected by the type(s) of attribute values projected (i.e., integer, string). The third set of tests measures the performance of a projection on all of the attributes versus a simple 'retrieve all' command.

After the time basic variables have been estimated, other performance factors are investigated. The use of indices can reduce access time. By reducing the amount of data brought into the memory, the processing time is also reduced. However, the processing time will be increased due to index access and search. Therefore, for some relations, the use of indices may increase the response time. Indexing

44

requires a specific set of tests to measure its performance in various situations. The use of different types of indices (i.e., clustered, non-clustered, multiple keys, etc.) must also be investigated. An expected factor in index performance is the ratio of the index size (in blocks of storage) to that of the relation.

String compression (removal of trailing spaces) is a factor which can affect the processing time, the access time and the return time. The use of compression can reduce block storage dramatically. This, in turn, reduces the access time. However, it may require more time to process a compressed string versus a non-compressed one, if processing requires expansion of the compressed attribute. If expansion is not required for processing, then the host may have to expand it for proper formatting. How expensive (in time) is this? Does this compensate for the reduction in the responnse time resulting from returning a smaller amount of data (the compressed string) to the host?.

Other performance factors may be examined eitner individually or within other test procedures. An example of this is the use of different types of attributes (i.e.. integer versus string). A complete series of tests can be developed to test this issue in detail. However, it is also appropriate to investigate this area in conjunction with processing time and projections.

45

2. Experiments Involving More Than One Relation

Operations involving more than one relation (i.e., joins) are affected by the same time variables as those involving only a single relation. Initial testing should involve only two relations.

It is expected that the access time will become dominant for join operations. This is because the same data may have to be accessed repeatedly. Memory size has an effect on the amount of accessing required in a join operation. If memory size is large enough to allow both relations to be accessed once and left in the memory, then the processing time may become significant. In this circumstance both the access time and the processing time are expected to increase proportionally to the relation size. The unknown factor is the rate at which the processing time increases. However, it may be that neither relation is small enough to be held in the memory for processing. In this case much accessing must be performed. It may also be of interest to examine join performance between these two extremes.

The join should be designed to take advantage of any size differential between the two relations. If the smaller relation can be completely held in the memory, then it can be accessed once and brought into the memory. The larger relation can also be accessed just once as it is brought into the memory as a stream. If, on the other hand, the

larger relation is brought into the memory, it must be brought into the memory a portion at a time. The smaller relation may have to be reaccessed for each portion of the larger relation.

It is important to examine the performance of joins both with and without selection. In performing these tests, the strategy of the operations should be examined carefully. The selection should be performed before the actual join operation to minimize the volume of data being joined.

Another area of interest is the effect of index usage on joins. Performance here is expected to improve as indicated by the single relation index experiments. However the specific results may suggest the efficiency with which the join operation has been implemented.

If inequality joins have been implemented, performance testing should be conducted using them. If they have not been implemented, it may be valuable to know if, and with what difficulty, they can be simulated.

Having experimented the join operations involving two relations, experiments operations should be conducted using larger numbers of relations in one join operation. By investigating the performance on multiple join relations, it may be possible to isolate a fixed overhead for all the initial joins.

3. A Flexible Test Plan

A general test plan should be developed before any of the experiments are designed. It should be flexible to enable testing to follow different paths of discovery. It is expected that the results of some experiments may suggest other experiments. Time must be alloted for the expansion of any test set.

However, it must also ensure that the a sufficient range of data is obtained. The tests must cover the universal operations (i.e., those expected of any DBMS). Among the universal operations, known bottlenecks and breakpoints are specifically tested. It should also investigate any specific strengths, weaknesses or idiosyncrasies of the DBMS.

B. MEASUREMENT TOOLS

The response-time measurements in these experiments were taken from the backend-machine clock. This clock has a resolution of 1/60 second and an accuracy within 1/60-th of a second. The response time of the backend machine on small relations is dominated by communications overhead. The minimum response time is about one second. So, of the tests conducted, the 1/60-second interval is sufficiently accurate.

However, if the overhead can be reduced, a more precise measuring device is required. Most mainframe operating systems provide a clock with a resolution in microseconds. This is not available in the backend machine.

C. QUERY SCRIPTS VERSUS PROGRAMS

Two methods exist for performing benchmark experiments. These methods involve the use of query scripts and programs. The first of these simulates an interactive session accessing the database. The actual terminal input is prepared ahead of time and stored in a 'run-stream' file, known as a query script. The host operating system can be instructed to obtain its input from a file instead of via the terminal. Thus a series of tests can be collected together in a script. Additionally the output can be redirected to a file, removing the overhead in communicating with a terminal.

The use of batch programs involves much more of the programmer's time in the development and debugging of the program. Development of batch programs also represent a larger drain on the host's resources. This factor could severely affect testing at many installations.

Since queries must be interpreted whether they come from a batch job or a script, the use of batch programming did not offer the advantages of bypassing the query processor. Therefore, there is some question whether or not a batch

program would provide superior performance results. This question and the ease of development of query scripts suggest that the use of query scripts is the desired method. If batch programming offers a significant performance improvement, additional testing must be performed using batch jobs. Here it would be wise to run a complete battery of tests in the interactive environment, followed by a subset of these tests in the batch environment. This subset should be designed to test areas where the batch process may have its most impact (i.e., the data return time).

D. INTERPRETING THE DATA

The interpretation of data is a very important part of the testing phase. There are two reasons for this. First, conclusions cannot be drawn from raw data. Second, Timely interpretation enables the persons conducting the experiments to analyze the results and identify further testing.

A collection of raw data is very hard to interpret. Therefore, any results obtained should be graphed immediately. Graphing the results immediately allows rapid identification of errors and unexpected results. Related results should also be graphed together. For example, all the results from a query applied to relations of different tuple length and relation size should be graphed together.

Once the raw data is analyzed, the graphs may be refined. The graph axes may be varied as appropriate. For

example, the response time may be graphed against the tuple length, against the relation size (in tuples or the number of blocks of the storage space occupied) and against the quantity of data returned to the user.

VI. CONCLUSIONS

A. RESULTS

The results obtained from testing several configurations of a relational database machine have provided a basis for developing a general set of benchmark tests for relational database machines. The benchmarking tests have been mostly machine independent. Although a testing methodology is provided herein with enough results on certain configurations, additional testing is necessary. This testing should be performed on other DBMSs, preferably with different characteristics, to ensure that the test is complete and not machine-specific. The results of testing selection and projection operations are described in [4]. Results from performing tests on join operations are described in [5].

1. General Results

The response time has been shwn to be proportional to the time required to access the data. This, in turn, has been shown to be proportional to physical size of the database. Methods used to reduce the amount of data to be brought into the memory for processing (such as indexing and string compression) improve the response time.

The response time is also proportional to the amount of data returned to the user. In the case of the RDM 1100, the time required to return the data is the largest

52

component of the total response time. If the necessary information is obtained via aggregate functions, the response time is greatly improved. It is not possible to determine how much of the response time is due to the back-end machine and how much is due to the host. However, loading the host definitely degrades the response time. An analysis of the response time under various load conditions in the host may lead to a distinction of the host response time vs. the backend response time.

The time required to process queries and the time required to process data in the memory are relatively small for the RDM 1100. This may not be true for other systems. Therefore, it is imperative that these areas be carefully examined when adapting the proposed tests to systems with different architectures.

The results of the experiments show that DBMSs do have characteristics which may be measured. A well-conceived series of tests can measure an installation's performance, and gain an indication of its performance and its 'personality.' These tests can be used to compare DBMSs against each other. For the DBMS implementor, the tests also provide a method of determining poorly implemented parts of the system.

2. Research Results

The experiments which have been performed have supported two different types of study. The first is the actual measurement of the backend machine's performance (albeit, with light load and few configurations). The RDM 1100 provides a comprehensive (although uncomplete) relational model which successfully offloads DEMS tasks from the host. Since evaluation of the machine was conducted simultaneously with the research, the task of evaluating it has been accomplished. Some areas that have not been fully investigated are due to the lack of time. Other areas that have not been fully investogated are due to incomplete implementation. As an example of these areas, the use of **ALL** in a retrieve s is contigent upon the number of attributes. At one point, the use of **ALL** on a relation with a large number of attributes results in only an error message. After installation of the accelerator, the use of **ALL** halts the command. After the accelerator is removed, the problem of halting persists. Another deficiency noted has been the inability to perform an inequality join.

B. A RELATIONAL BENCHMARKING METHODOLOGY

The proposed set of benchmark tests has four phases. The first phase consists of preliminary tests designed to identify the best method of measuring the system's response time. The second phase involves isolating the different

components of the response time. The third phase investigates the system response in specific areas. The fourth phases verifies the results obtained during the phases two and three.

1. <u>Phase One</u> − <u>Measurement Methods</u>

Most systems have at least one mechanism which provides a time measurement. Initial testing is designed to identify the one which optimize the precision obtained versus the ease of obtaining that time. Once the measurement method has been chosen, it is checked to ensure that it is accurate enough to provide the necessary precision. It is also necessary to ensure that the overhead involved in retrieving the time does not reduce the precision of the measurements being taken.

If the necessary precision is not readily available, then techniques are available to increase the precision of the results. These techniques involve performing an operation several times and calculating an average. The techniques selected must be reviewed for side effects. The DBMS may have the capability of internally optimizing performance. For example, the order in which the queries are submitted to the DBMS may allow the DBMS cache memory management to reduce disk access.

In the case of the RDM 1100, two different methods of measuring time could have been used. The first method is to obtain a time stamp from the host operating system.

Although it may have provided sufficient precision, it has not been investigated because of the other methods available. The second method is a time stamp available from the IDM. A built-in function supplies an elapsed time measurement intervals of one-sixtieth of a second. This provides sufficient precision for the measurements. Since the elapsed time is a sufficient measurement, the more precise measurement has not been used.

    2. <u>Phase</u> <u>Two</u> - <u>Component</u> <u>Isolation</u>

        Once an adequate method for measuring time has been verified, it is used to measure the performance in several specific areas. These areas are the four components which are involved in all queries: the time of process the query (i.e., parse it), the time to access the data in the database, the time to process the data in the memory, and the time to return the requested. These components may be considered the DBMS'S primitive operations. These primitives do not take advantage of any methods used to improve the response time of a given query. They merely measure the performance of the hardware and software in performing specific functions. It has been stated that a performance measurement of some aspects of a DBMS is really a measurement of the operating system. The operating system does effect DBMS response. However, in the case of a backend machine, this effect is minimal for some operations. While

56

this issue may be debated, it is not of interest to the user. The user is not interested in the reasons why a system responds poorly. He is interested only in the fact that a system performs properly and the fact that the system's performance is better (or worse) than that of another system. He is most interested in the possibility of obtaining a quicker response time on his application.

The system primitives are measured by a set of queries which isolate different aspects of the response time. One set of queries is designed to return the same amount of data from relations with the same number of tuples, but having different tuple sizes. Once a tuple is in the memory, it takes the same amount of time to project one attribute from a set of 100-byte tuples as from a set of 2000-byte tuples. The difference in the response time for the two queries is due only to the time necessary to bring the tuple into the memory. The times required to process the query, to process the data and to return the data are the same.

The second set of queries is designed to measure the time required to return the data to the user. These queries return a different amount of data (in bytes) from projection operations on the same number of attributes in the same format (i.e., strings, etc.) in relations which are of the

same physical size. These restrictions assure that the access time is the same, the processing time is the same, and the query processing time is the same.

The third set of queries is designed to isolate data processing time. In this set, the queries return the same amount of data from relations of the same physical size (i.e., identical storage requirements) but having a different number of tuples. This provides a measurement of the processing required relative to the number of tuples processed. The query processing time, the data access time, and the data return time are the same.

The fourth set of queries provides a measurement of query processing time. For operations on relations of any significant size, this is hard to measure. Even on small relations, it may not be significant compared to simple system overhead. This set of queries is more complex than the previous sets. The queries are constructed to allow the effects of the time elements (i.e., the three just measured) to be subtracted from the measurements, leaving only the query processing time. Considering the difficulty in obtaining a precise measurement of the query processing time, it may not be worthwhile to determine this value because of its small size.

The previous discussion indicates that the query sets are independent. However, with proper planning the query sets may be combined with equivalent results. In the

graph shown in Figure 3, one set of experiments provides a measurement of data access times and data return times. The set also isolates the constant query overhead (which includes the query processing time).

Figure 3 represents the response time of two queries. One query selects five percent of the tuples and returns all of the attribute fields from each tuple. The second query is identical except that it selects ten percent of the tuples. The queries are both run against relations with 100-byte tuples. The relations vary in size from 500 tuples to 10,000 tuples. Point A on the graph represents the five percent selection on 10,000 tuples. Point B represents the ten percent selection on 5000 tuples. Since each of these queries returns 500 tuples, the time to return the data is the same. The overhead associated with each query, including query processing time, is the same. Therefore, the difference between the response times represented by Points A and B is the difference is the access time and the processing time of the queries. Point A represents a retrieve on 10,000 tuples, which is 500 blocks of disk storage. Point B represents a retrieve on 5000 tuples, or 250 disk blocks. Assuming that processing time for these queries is insignificant relative to the access time, fore, the difference in the two response times is the time to access 250 disk blocks.

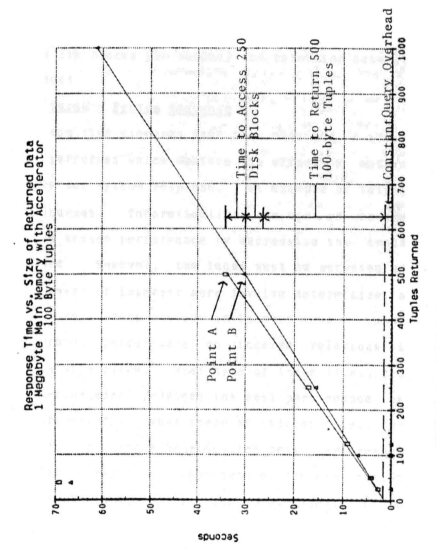

FIGURE 3 - RESPONSE TIME VS. SIZE OF RETURNED DATA

60

The overhead for all the queries shown on the graph is the same and is represented by the common intercept of the vertical axis. If the time represented by Point F is adjusted for the overhead and the time to access 250 blocks, then the result is the time to return 500 100-byte tuples. Therefore, the use of one query set has identified rates for accessing data (in blocks per second) and returning data (in bytes per second)

3. Phase Three - System Response

After the time elements have been measured, a set of queries are performed which measure the effect of methods used to improve the system response. An example of this is the use of indexes. Theoretically, the use of indexes should improve system performance by decreasing the amount of data accessed. However, the index must be accessed and processed. Areas of interest here involve determining at what point, if any, does the use of indexes become important. Therefore, performance on indexed relations is measured over a wide range. What type of index (i.e., clustered or non-clustered) provides the best performance and what are the trade-offs? What scope of indices (i.e., one attribute, two, or more) provides the best performance? The latter question may be one dependent on the application. In testing the RDM 1100, it has been noted that, if the index is defined when the relation is being created, then the size of a relation with a clustered index is larger then

61

the size of the same relation if the index is defined after
the data has been entered into the relation. This is because the loading algorithm assumes a normal distribution of
key values, while the data is in key sequence. data loaded
has been generated already sorted.

Additional testing should be performed to get a
'feel' of the system. By becoming familiar with the system's capabilities, the testing personnel should be able to
determine interesting lines of experimentation. Areas of
interest include the overhead associated with projection
operations, the use of string compression techniques, and
the efficiency of join operations (in different available
memory configurations, when available).

4. <u>Phase Four - Verification</u>

The last phase takes place after the other tests
have been reviewed and graphed. Analysis of the previous
tests should provide some meaningful results about system
performance in general, and in particular areas. The veri-
fication phase serves to perform tests which verify or
disprove the analysis of the previous tests. It also provides an opportunity to redo any tests which appear errone-
ous or suspicious. In this phase, additional tests may take
advantage of the flexibility designed into the synthetic
database.

C. SUMMARY

Investigation of the performance of several configurations of a backend relational database machine has provided considerable insight into what may be a sound basis for general performance testing on relational DBMSs. In this thesis, a methodology has been laid out and the initial phases to be taken in that methodology have been defined. A complete framework for subsequent phases has not been fully developed, but their contents have been discussed. While the tests described relate to a specific series of relational database machines, the basic methodology may apply to relational database machines.

IDM System Tables

System Tables

1. Databases - catalog of databases in the system

2. Disks - list of disks known to system

3. Lock - used by IDM for concurrency control

4. Configure - information about serial and parallel interfaces, checkpoint interval

5. DBinstat - information about current activity in the IDM

Database Tables

1. Relation - catalog of all objects (relation, view, stored command) in the database

2. Attribute - catalog of each attribute of each relation

3. Indices - catalog of indices that exist in the database

4. Protect - catalog of protection information in the database

5. Query - stored commands and view

6. Crossreference - catalog of dependencies among relations, views and stored commands

7. Transact - transaction logging relation

8. Users - mapping of user and group names to user ID

9. Host_Users - mapping from host ID and user ID to IDM ID

10. Blockalloc - catalog of disk blocks

11. Disk_Usage - database allocation

12. Batch - temporary transaction logging relation

13. Descriptions - user definable descriptions

```
PROGRAM GR2014;

(* THIS IS THE VM/CMS VERSION OF THE RELATION GENERATOR (RG).  RG PROMPTS THE
USER FOR INFORMATION ABOUT A RELATION: NAME, NUMBER OF TUPLES, ATTRIBUTES, AND
ATTRIBUTE TYPES.  ATTRIBUTE VALUES ARE GENERATED ONE AT A TIME BASED ON THE U-
SER'S INPUT.  AFTER ALL ATTRIBUTE VALUES HAVE BEEN GENERATED, THEN THE RELATION
ITSELF IS CREATED. *)

CONST   NUMBER_OF_ATTRIBUTES = 25;
        NAME_LENGTH = 8;
        FILE_NAME_LENGTH = 17;
        STR_LEN = 25;
        LRECL = 2034;

TYPE    NAME = STRING (8);
        ATTRIBUTE_TYPE = PACKED ARRAY (.1..2.) OF CHAR;
        ARRAY_OF_PROPORTIONS = ARRAY (.1..20.) OF INTEGER;
        ATTR_REC = RECORD (* ATTRIBUTE DESCRIPTION RECORD *)
            ATTR_NAME : NAME;
            ATTR_TYPE : ATTRIBUTE_TYPE;
            STRINGLENGTH : INTEGER;
            LOWER_BOUND : INTEGER;
            UPPER_BOUND : INTEGER;
            GEN_MODE : INTEGER;
            VALUE_SET_NAME : NAME;
            REL_PROPORTIONS : ARRAY_OF_PROPORTIONS;
            SEED : INTEGER
        END;
        ALPH = SET OF CHAR;
        ATTR_ARRAY = ARRAY (.1..NUMBER_OF_ATTRIBUTES.) OF ATTR_REC;

VAR     DONE,RELATIONS_DONE_ATTRIBUTES, GOOD_ANSWER : BOOLEAN;
        TTYIN,TTYOUT : TEXT;   (* PASCAL/VS TERMINAL IDENTIFIERS *)
        ANSWER : CHAR;
        RELATION_NAME : NAME;
        TEMP_STRING : STRING (20);
        GOOD_LETTER : ALPH;
        I,SIZE,TEST,ATTR_CREATED,VALU ,TYPE_SIZE,RELATION_SIZE,TOTAL : INTEGER;
        ATTR_INFC : ATTR_ARRAY;

PROCEDURE ENTER_INT ( VAR SUM : INTEGER );

(* READS A NUMBER FROM THE USER AS A CHARACTER STRING, THEN CONVERTS IT TO A
WHOLE NUMBER.  IF A NON INTEGER IS ENTERED THE PROCEDURE WILL NOT ACCEPT IT
AND ASKS FOR ANOTHER NUMBER. *)
```

```
VAR TEMP : STRING (80);
    NUMBER : SET CF CHAR;
    I : INTEGER;
    ERROR : BCCLEAN;

BEGIN
  NUMBER := ('.','0'..'9',' ',',','-');
  REPEAT
    READLN (TTYIN,TEMP);
    ERROR := FALSE;
    IF LENGTH (TEMP) > 0 THEN
      BEGIN
        IF LENGTH (TEMP) > 15 THEN (* TRUNCATE TO 15 CHARACTERS *)
          TEMP := SUBSTR (TEMP,1,15);
        FCR I := 1 TC LENGTH (TEMP) CO (* CHECK FOR BAD CHARACTER *)
          IF NOT(TEMP (.I.) IN NUMBER) THEN
            ERROR := TRUE;
        IF ERROR THEN
          WRITELN (TTYOUT, 'INCORRECT INPUT.  ENTER AN INTEGER ',
                          'VALUE ONLY.  TRY AGAIN.')

      END
    ELSE (* NIL ENTRY *)
      BEGIN
        ERROR := TRUE;
        WRITELN (TTYOUT, 'YOU MUST ENTER AN INTEGER.  TRY AGAIN.')

      END
  UNTIL NOT (ERROR);
  WRITELN (TEMP);
  READSTR (TEMP, SUM)
END;

PROCEDURE GET_NAME (VAR FILE_NAME : NAME);

(* READS A VALIC FILE NAME FRCM THE TERMINAL *)

  VAR GOOD_ANSWER, FLAG : BOOLEAN;
      I : INTEGER;
      TEMP : STRING (80);

BEGIN
  GOOD_ANSWER := FALSE;
  REPEAT
    READLN (TTYIN, TEMP_STRING);
    IF LENGTH (TEMP_STRING) = 0 THEN
      WRITELN (TTYCUT, 'YOU MUST ENTER A NAME.')
    ELSE
      IF TEMP_STRING (.1.) = ' ' THEN
```

66

```
        ELSE WRITELN (TTYOUT, 'PLEASE DO NOT START WITH A BLANK TRY AGAIN.')
        BEGIN
          IF LENGTH (TEMP_STRING) > 8 THEN
             TEMP_STRING := SUBSTR (TEMP_STRING, 1, 8);
          I := 0;
          FLAG := FALSE;
          REPEAT
             I := I + 1;
             IF NOT (TEMP_STRING (.I.) IN GOOD_LETTER) THEN
                BEGIN
                   WRITELN(TTYOUT,'PLEASE USE LETTERS ONLY.  TRY AGAIN.');
                   FLAG := TRUE
                END
          UNTIL (I = LENGTH (TEMP_STRING)) OR FLAG;
          GOOD_ANSWER := NOT FLAG;
        END ANSWER;
     WRITELN (TEMP_STRING);
     FILE_NAME := TEMP_STRING
END;

PROCEDURE GET_RELATION_NAME (VAR RELATION_NAME : NAME);

   (* PROMPTS THE USER FOR THE RELATION NAME *)

BEGIN
   WRITELN (TTYOUT, 'INPUT THE DESIRED NAME FOR THIS RELATION (MAXIMUM OF 8 ',
            'CHARACTERS).-');
   GET_NAME (RELATION_NAME)
END;

PROCEDURE GET_RELATION_SIZE (VAR RELATION_SIZE : INTEGER);

   (* PROMPTS THE USER FOR THE NUMBER OF TUPLES IN THE RELATION. *)

   VAR
      GOOD_ANSWER : BOOLEAN;

BEGIN
   WRITELN (TTYOUT);
   WRITELN (TTYOUT, 'ENTER THE SIZE OF THE RELATION.');
   REPEAT
      ENTER INT (RELATION_SIZE);
      IF RELATION_SIZE < 1 THEN
         BEGIN
            WRITELN (TTYOUT, 'INCORRECT INPUT.  THE NUMBER OF RELATIONS MUST ',
```

```
                 'BE GREATER THAN ).');
       ELSE
          GOOD_ANSWER := TRUE
    END
  UNTIL GOOD_ANSWER
END;

PROCEDURE GET_ATTRIBUTE_NAME (VAR ATTR_NAME : NAME);

(* PROMPTS THE USER FOR AN ATTRIBUTE NAME. *)

BEGIN
  WRITELN (TTYOUT, 'ENTER THE NAME OF THE ATTRIBUTE (MAXIMUM OF 8 LETTERS).',
           'THIS IS ATTRIBUTE');
  WRITELN (TTYOUT, 'NUMBER ',ATTR_CREATED :2,' OF RELATION "',
           RELATION_NAME,'". THE MAXIMUM NUMBER OF ATTRIBUTES ALLOWED IS',
           NUMBER_OF_ATTRIBUTES :3,'.');
  GET_NAME (ATTR_NAME)
END;

PROCEDURE GET_ATTRIBUTE_TYPE (VAR ATTR_TYPE : ATTRIBUTE_TYPE);

(* PROMPTS THE USER FOR THE TYPE OF ATTRIBUTE. ACCEPTS ONLY VALID TYPES. *)

VAR
  GOOD_ANSWER : BOOLEAN;

BEGIN
  WRITELN (TTYOUT, 'ENTER ATTRIBUTE TYPE.');
  WRITELN (TTYOUT);
  WRITELN (TTYOUT, '  C  -- CHARACTER STRING (COMPRESSED).');
  WRITELN (TTYOUT, '  UC -- CHARACTER STRING (UNCOMPRESSED).');
  WRITELN (TTYOUT, '  I1 -- INTEGER (1 BYTE).');
  WRITELN (TTYOUT, '  I2 -- INTEGER (2 BYTES).');
  WRITELN (TTYOUT, '  I4 -- INTEGER (4 BYTES).');
  GOOD_ANSWER := FALSE;
  REPEAT (* UNTIL GOOD_ANSWER *)
    ATTR_TYPE (.2.) := ' ';
    READ (TTYIN, ATTR_TYPE (.1.));
    IF NOT EOLN (TTYIN) THEN
      READLN (TTYIN, ATTR_TYPE (.2.));
    IF ((ATTR_TYPE (.1.) IN (.'C','U'.)) AND (ATTR_TYPE (.2.) = ' '))
      OR ((ATTR_TYPE (.1.) IN (.'U','C'.)) AND (ATTR_TYPE(.2.) IN (.'C','C'.)))
```

```
               ((ATTR_TYPE(.1.))IN (.'I','I'.)) AND (ATTR_TYPE(.2.) IN (.'1','2','4'.)))
          ELSE GOOD_ANSWER := TRUE
               WRITELN (TTYOUT,'I              .       E       C, UC, I1, I2      I4      .';
               T
     UNTIL GOOD_ANSWER;
     WRITELN (ATTR_TYPE)
END;

PROCEDURE GET_STRING_LENGTH (VAR STRING_LENGTH : INTEGER);

(* PROMPTS THE USER FOR LENGTH OF A STRING ATTRIBLTE. *)

VAR
     GOOD_ANSWER : BOOLEAN;

BEGIN
     WRITELN (TTYOUT);
     WRITELN (TTYOUT,'INPUT LENGTH OF STRINGS TO BE USED (1-255).');
     REPEAT
          ENTER INT (STRING_LENGTH);
          IF (STRING_LENGTH< 1) OR (STRING_LENGTH > 255) THEN
          BEGIN
               GOOD_ANSWER := FALSE;
               WRITELN (TTYOUT,'INCORRECT INPUT.  STRING LENGTH MUST BE BETWEEN',
                    ' 1 AND 255.  TRY AGAIN.')
          END
          ELSE
               GOOD_ANSWER := TRUE
     UNTIL GOOD_ANSWER
END;

PROCEDURE GET_MODE (FLAG_CHAR : CHAR; VAR GEN_MODE : INTEGER);

(* PROMPTS USER FOR THE MODE TO BE USED IN GENERATING AN ATTRIBUTE. WILL NOT
ACCEPT AN IMPROPER MODE. *)

VAR
     GOOD_ANSWER : BOOLEAN;
     LAST : INTEGER;

BEGIN
     LAST := 3;
     WRITELN (TTYOUT);
     WRITELN (TTYOUT,'ENTER DESIRED MODE FOR GENERATION OF DATA:');
     WRITELN (TTYOUT);
```

```
WRITELN (TTYOUT,' 1:: INTEGERS SEQUENTIALLY OVER A GIVEN RANGE.');
WRITELN (TTYOUT,' 2:: INTEGERS PSEUDO-RANDOMLY OVER A GIVEN RANGE.');
WRITELN (TTYOUT,' 3:: UNIQUE INTEGERS PSEUDO-RANDOMLY OVER A GIVEN RANGE.');
IF NOT (FLAG_CHAR IN ('1','2','3','4','5','6')) THEN
   BEGIN
     WRITELN (TTYOUT,' 4 :: CHARACTERS IN COLLATING SEQUENCE.');
     WRITELN (TTYOUT,' 5 :: INTEGERS OR CHARACTERS SELECTED PSEUDO-',
       'RANDOMLY FROM GIVEN SETS.');
     WRITELN (TTYOUT,'6:: INTEGERS OR CHARACTERS SELECTED ACCORDING TO A',
       'GIVEN DISTRIBUTION FROM');
     WRITELN (TTYOUT,' PREDEFINED SETS.');
     LAST := 6
   END;
REPEAT
  ENTER INT (GEN_MODE);
  IF (GEN_MODE < 1) OR (GEN_MODE > 6) THEN
     BEGIN
       GOOD_ANSWER := FALSE;
       WRITELN (TTYOUT,'INCORRECT INPUT. GENERATION MODE MUST BE ',
         'BETWEEN 1 AND 6. TRY AGAIN.')
     END
  ELSE
     GOOD_ANSWER := TRUE
UNTIL GOOD_ANSWER
END;

PROCEDURE GET_RANGE (INT_TYPE : CHAR; VAR LOW, HIGH : INTEGER);

(* PROMPTS THE USER FOR THE RANGE OF RANDOM INTEGER ATTRIBUTES. *)

VAR
   GOOD_ANSWER : BOOLEAN;
   VALU, LOWER_BOUND, UPPER_BOUND : INTEGER;

BEGIN
  CASE INT_TYPE OF
    '1' : BEGIN
            LOWER_BOUND := -128;
            UPPER_BOUND := 127
          END;
    '2' : BEGIN
            LOWER_BOUND := -32768;
            UPPER_BOUND := 32767
          END;
    '4' : BEGIN
            LOWER_BOUND := -2140000000;
            UPPER_BOUND := 2140000000
          END
```

70

```pascal
END;(* CASE *)
WRITELN (TTYOUT, 'ENTER THE LOWER BOUND TO BE USED FOR THIS ATTRIBUTE.',
  ' ', LIMITS, ' ARE ', TO ',LOWER_BOUND);
GOOD_ANSWER := FALSE;
REPEAT
  ENTER INT (LOW);
  IF (LOW < LOWER_BOUND) OR (LOW > UPPER_BOUND) THEN
    WRITELN(TTYOUT,'INCORRECT INPUT. ENTRY IS OUT OF BOUNDS. ',
      'TRY AGAIN.')
  ELSE
    GOOD_ANSWER := TRUE
UNTIL GOOD_ANSWER;
WRITELN (TTYOUT, 'ENTER THE UPPER-BOUND TO BE USED FOR THIS ATTRIBUTE.',
  ' ', LIMITS, ' ARE ', TO ',LOW);, UPPER_BOUND);
GOOD_ANSWER := FALSE;
REPEAT
  ENTER INT (HIGH);
  IF (HIGH < LOW) OR (HIGH > UPPER_BOUND) THEN
    WRITELN (TTYOUT,'INCORRECT INPUT. ENTRY IS OUT OF BOUNDS. ',
      'TRY AGAIN.')
  ELSE
    GOOD_ANSWER := TRUE
UNTIL GOOD_ANSWER
END;

PROCEDURE GET_VALUE_SET_DATA (VAR VALUE_SET_NAME : NAME;
                             VAR LOWER_BOUND, UPPER_BOUND : INTEGER);

(* PROMPTS THE USER FOR DATA ABOUT A VALUE SET TO BE USED IN GENERATING AN
   ATTRIBUTE. *)

VAR
  TEMP_STRING : STRING (80);
  GOOD_ANSWER : BOOLEAN;
  I : INTEGER;

BEGIN
  WRITELN (TTYOUT);
  WRITELN (TTYOUT, 'ENTER THE NAME OF THE FILE CONTAINING THE VALUE SET. ',
    'ENSURE THAT THIS FILE EXISTS.');
  WRITELN(TTYOUT,'EXISTS.');
  GET NAME (VALUE_SET_NAME);
  WRITELN (TTYOUT);
  WRITELN (TTYOUT, 'ENTER THE NUMBER OF VALUES IN ', VALUE_SET_NAME ,
    'VALUES THAT YOU WILL BE USING FOR');
  WRITELN (TTYOUT, 'THIS ATTRIBUTE.');
```

71

```
REPEAT
  ENTER_INT (UPPER_BOUND);
  IF (UPPER_BOUND < 1) OR (UPPER_BOUND > 255) THEN
    BEGIN
      GOOD_ANSWER := FALSE;
      WRITELN (TTYOUT,'INCORRECT INPUT.  ENTRY MUST BE > 0 AND < 20.',
      ' TRY AGAIN.')
    END
  ELSE
    GOOD_ANSWER := TRUE
UNTIL GOOD_ANSWER;
LOWER_BOUND := 1
END;

PROCEDURE GET_PROPORTIONS (VAR PROPORTIONS : ARRAY_OF_PROPORTIONS;
                           UPPER_BOUND : INTEGER);

(* PROMPTS THE USER FOR THE PROPORTIONS TO BE USED IN GENERATING AN ATTRIBUTE
FROM A VALUE SET. *)

VAR
  DONE_PROPORTIONS : BOOLEAN;
  SIZE : INTEGER;

BEGIN
  WRITELN (TTYOUT,'ENTER THE RELATIVE PROPORTIONS TO BE USED FOR GENERATING',
  WRITELN (TTYOUT,'THIS ATTRIBUTE FROM.');    THESE PROPORTIONS MUST CORRESPOND TO',
  WRITELN (TTYOUT,'EACH ENTRY TO BE USED.');    THE PROPORTIONS MUST BE MULTIPLES OF ',
  WRITELN (TTYOUT,'FIVE.  ENSURE THAT THE');
                  'NUMBER OF ENTRIES FROM')  PROPORTIONS IS EQUAL TO OR LESS THAN THE ',
  WRITELN (TTYOUT);
  WRITELN (TTYOUT);    'THE FILE TO BE USED.');
  TOTAL := 0;
  SIZE := 0;
  DONE_PROPORTIONS := FALSE;
  REPEAT
    WRITELN (TTYOUT,'INPUT THE NEXT PROPORTION:');
    ENTER_INT (VALU);
    IF VALU MOD 5 <> 0 THEN
      WRITELN (TTYOUT,'INCORRECT INPUT.    PROPORTION MUST BE A MULTIPLE ',
      'OF FIVE.  TRY AGAIN.')
    ELSE (VALU + TOTAL) > 100 THEN
      BEGIN
        WRITELN (TTYOUT, 'ERROR - THE LAST INPUT HAS BEEN ',
```

```
                'DISREGARDED.  THE TOTAL EXCEEDED 100%.');
    ELSE WRITELN (TTYOUT, 'TRY AGAIN.')
    ELSE (* TOTAL + VALU < 100% *)
        BEGIN
        SIZE := SIZE + 1;
        PROPORTIONS (.SIZE.) := VALU;
        TOTAL := TOTAL + VALU;
        IF TOTAL = 100 THEN
          IF UPPER_BOUND = SIZE THEN
            DONE_PROPORTIONS := TRUE
          ELSE (* UPPER_BOUND > SIZE *)
            BEGIN
            WRITELN (TTYOUT, 'PRESENT TOTAL =100%, BUT NOT ALL ',
                     'ENTRIES ARE REPRESENTED.  START OVER.');
            TOTAL := 0;
            SIZE := 0;
            END
        ELSE
          IF SIZE < UPPER_BOUND THEN
            WRITELN (TTYOUT, 'PRESENT TOTAL IS', TOTAL : 4, '%.')
          ELSE
            BEGIN
            WRITELN (TTYOUT, 'ALL VALUE SET FILE ENTRIES WHICH ',
                     'ARE TO BE REPRESENTED HAVE BEEN ASSIGNED');
            WRITELN (TTYOUT, 'PROPORTIONS, BUT THE TOTAL DOESN'T ',
                     'EQUAL 100%.  START OVER.');
            TOTAL := 0;
            SIZE := 0;
            END
  UNTIL DONE_PROPORTIONS
END;

PROCEDURE GENERATE (IN_REC : ATTR_REC; NUMBER_TO_GENERATE : INTEGER);

(* THIS PROCEDURE CALLS A SUBPROCEDURE TO GENERATE AN ATTRIBUTE VALUE LIST,
   THEN STORES THE LIST IN A FILE. *)

TYPE
  MARKP = @INTEGER;
  I_POINTER = @I_NODE;
  I_NODE = RECORD
           I_VAL : INTEGER;
           LINK : I_POINTER
           END;
  C_POINTER = @C_NODE;
  C_NODE =
```

73

```
  C_VAL : STRING(255);
  LINK : C_PCINTER
END;

VAR
B            :  MARKP;
IPTR1        :  I_PCINTER;
CPTR1        :  C_PCINTER;
VAL_NR       :  INTEGER;
SET_VAL      :  STRING(STR_LEN);
ATTR_NR      :  INTEGER;
OUTFILE      :  TEXT;
NAME_OF_FILE :  STRING (25);
STRFILE      :  FILE OF STRING (STR_LEN);

PROCEDURE INI_SEQLENTIAL (IN_REC : ATTR_REC; RELATION_SIZE : INTEGER;
        VAR TOP_OF_LIST : I_POINTER);

(* GENERATES A LIST OF INTEGERS IN NUMERICALLY SEQUENTIAL ORDER. *)

VAR
  I : INTEGER;
  CUR_NODE : I_POINTER;

BEGIN (TCP_CF_LIST);
NEW (TCP_CF_LIST);
CUR_NODE := TOP_OF_LIST;
CUR_NODE@.I_VAL := IN_REC.LOWER_BOUND;
IF RELATION_SIZE > 1 THEN
   FOR I:=IN_REC.LOWER_BOUND+ 1 TO IN_REC.LOWER_BOUND + RELATION_SIZE - 1 DO
      BEGIN
      NEW (CUR_NODE@.LINK);
      CUR_NODE := CUR_NODE@.LINK;
      CUR_NODE@.I_VAL := I
      END;
CUR_NODE@.LINK := NIL
END;

PROCEDURE INTRANDOM (IN_REC : ATTR_REC; ATTR_NR : INTEGER; VAR ANSWER
        : I_POINTER);

(* GENERATES A LIST OF RANDOM NUMBERS WITHIN A SPECIFIED RANGE. *)

VAR
  NUM, I, LOW, HIGH : INTEGER;
  P,Q : I_PCINTER;
  RND_NBR, REAL_NUM : REAL;
```

74

```
BEGIN
  LOW := IN_REC.LOWER_BOUND;
  HIGH := IN_REC.UPPER_BOUND;
  RND_NBR := RANDOM (IN_REC. SEED);
  REAL_NUM := ROUND ((LOW - RND_NBR * LOW) + RND_NBR * HIGH);
  NUM := ROUND (REAL_NUM);
  NEW (P);
  ANSWER := P;
  P@.IVAL := NUM;
  FOR I := 2 TO ATTR_NR DO
    BEGIN
      RND_NBR := RANDOM (0);
      REAL_NUM := (LOW - RND_NBR * LOW) + RND_NBR * HIGH;
      NUM := ROUND (REAL_NUM);
      NEW (Q);
      P@.LINK := Q;
      P := Q;
      P@.IVAL := NUM;
      IF I = ATTR_NR THEN
        P@.LINK := NIL
END; (* INTRANDOM *)

PROCEDURE INT_UNIQUE_RANDOM (IN_REC : ATTR_REC; ATTR_NR : INTEGER;
                             VAR ANSWER : I_POINTER);

(* GENERATES A LIST OF UNIQUE, RANDOM NUMBERS WITHIN A GIVEN RANGE. *)

TYPE
  T_PTR = @T_NODE;
  T_NODE = RECORD
    IVAL : INTEGER;
    LOW,FIR : T_PTR;
    HIGH_PTR : T_PTR
  END;

VAR
  BOTTOM, STORAGE,TREE : I_POINTER;
  SEARCH_TREE, NEXT_FTR, LAST_PTR : T_PTR;
  NUM, I, LOW, HIGH : INTEGER;
  RND_NBR, REAL_NUM : REAL;
  LOW_FLAG : BOOLEAN;

FUNCTION UNIQUE (NUM : INTEGER; VAR LOW : BOOLEAN) : BOOLEAN;

(* DETERMINES IF A VALUE IS ALREADY ON THE SEARCH TREE TO ENSURE THAT IT IS
```

75

```
UNIQUE. *)

  VAR
    IS_UNIQUE : BOOLEAN;

BEGIN
  NEXT_PTR := SEARCH_TREE;
  IS_UNIQUE := TRUE;
  WHILE (NEXT_PTR <> NIL) AND IS_UNIQUE DO
    IF NEXT_PTR@.I_VAL = NUM THEN
      IS_UNIQUE := FALSE
    ELSE
      BEGIN
        LAST_PTR := NEXT_PTR;
        IF NEXT_PTR@.I_VAL > NUM THEN
          BEGIN
            LOW := TRUE;
            NEXT_PTR := NEXT_PTR@.LOW_PTR
          END
        ELSE
          BEGIN
            LOW := FALSE;
            NEXT_PTR := NEXT_PTR@.HIGH_PTR
          END
      END;
  UNIQUE := IS_UNIQUE
END;

PROCEDURE STORE_SEARCH_TREE (NUM : INTEGER; LOW : BOOLEAN);

(* STORES A VALUE ON THE SEARCH TREE. *)

BEGIN
  IF LOW THEN
    BEGIN
      NEW(LAST_PTR@.LOW_PTR);
      NEXT_PTR := LAST_PTR@.LOW_PTR
    END
  ELSE
    BEGIN
      NEW(LAST_PTR@.HIGH_PTR);
      NEXT_PTR := LAST_PTR@.HIGH_PTR
    END;
  NEXT_PTR@.I_VAL := NUM;
  NEXT_PTR@.LOW_PTR := NIL;
  NEXT_PTR@.HIGH_PTR := NIL
END;
```

```
PROCEDURE STORE_STORAGE_TREE (NUM : INTEGER);

(* STORES A VALUE ON A SEARCH TREE. *)

BEGIN
  NEW(BOTTOM@.LINK);
  BOTTOM := BOTTOM@.LINK;
  BOTTOM@.I_VAL := NUM.
END;

BEGIN (* INT_UNIQUE_RANDOM *)
  LOW := IN_REC.LOWER_BOUND;
  HIGH := IN_REC.UPPER_BOUND;
  RND_NBR := IN_RANDOM (IN_REC.SEED);
  REAL_NUM := ROUND (LOW - LOW * RND_NBR) + HIGH * RND_NBR ;
  NUM := ROUND (REAL_NUM);
  NEW(ANSWER);
  STORAGE-TREE@ := ANSWER;
  STORAGE-TREE@.I_VAL := NUM;
  BOTTOM := STORAGE_TREE;
  NEW(SEARCH_TREE);
  SEARCH-TREE@.I_VAL := NUM;
  SEARCH-TREE@.LOW_PTR := NIL;
  SEARCH-TREE@.HIGH_PTR := NIL;
  NEXT_PTR := SEARCH_TREE;
  FOR I := 2 TO ATTR_NR DO
    BEGIN
      RND_NBR := RANDOM (0);
      NUM := (LOW - LOW * RND_NBR) + HIGH * RND_NBR;
      NUM := ROUND (REAL_NUM);
      WHILE NOT (UNIQUE (NUM, LOW_FLAG)) DO
        IF NUM := HIGH THEN

          ELSE
            NUM := NUM + 1;
        STORE_SEARCH_TREE (NUM, LOW_FLAG);
      STORE_STORAGE_TREE (NUM)

  END;
  BOTTOM@.LINK := NIL
END; (* INT_UNIQUE_RANDOM *)


PROCEDURE CHAR_SEC (IN_REC : ATTR_REC; RELATION_SIZE : INTEGER;
  VAR TOP_OF_LIST : C_POINTER);

(* GENERATES A LIST OF CHARACTER STRINGS IN ALPHABETICAL ORDER. *)

VAR
```

77

```
            LAST_CHAR: CHAR;
            FIRST_CHARS : STRING(255);
      I  :INTEGER;
            BOTTOM_OF_LIST : C_POINTER;
            CURRENT_STRING :: STRING (255);

FUNCTION GET_C_VAL (C_VAL : STRING(255)) : STRING (255);

(* GENERATES A CHARACTER STRINGS ALPHABETICAL SUCCESSOR. *)

     VAR
         LEN : INTEGER;

FUNCTION SUC (A_CHAR : CHAR ) : STRING(255);

(* OBTAINS A STRINGS ALPHABETICAL SUCCESSOR, INSPITE OF EBCDIC  *)

BEGIN
     REPEAT
          A_CHAR := SUCC (A_CHAR)
     UNTIL A_CHAR IN GOOD_LETTER;
     SUC := STR (A_CHAR)
END;

BEGIN (* GET(C_VAL *)
     LEN := LENGTH (C_VAL);
     IF (* LEN = 0 THEN DO NOTHING ELSE IF *)
        LEN <> 0 THEN
          BEGIN
              LAST_CHAR := C_VAL(.LEN.);
              FIRST_CHARS := SUBSTR(C_VAL, 1, LEN - 1);
              IF LAST_CHAR = 'Z' THEN
                 GET_C_VAL := GET_C_VAL (FIRST_CHARS) || STR ('A')
              ELSE
                 GET_C_VAL := FIRST_CHARS || SUC (LAST_CHAR)
          END

END;

PROCEDURE APPEND_STRING (CURRENT_STRING : STRING(255); VAR BOTTOM_OF_LIST :
          C_POINTER);

(* APPENDS A STRING TO THE BOTTOM OF THE LIST. *)

BEGIN
     NEW (BOTTOM_OF_LIST@.LINK);
     BOTTOM_OF_LIST := BOTTOM_OF_LIST@.LINK;
     BOTTOM_OF_LIST@.C_VAL := CURRENT_STRING
END;
```

78

```
BEGIN (* TCP CHAR SEQ *)
  NEW (TOP_CF_LIST);
  CURRENT_STRING := '';
  FOR I:= 1 TO IN_REC.STRING_LENGTH DO
    CURRENT_STRING := CURRENT_STRING || 'A';
  BOTTOM_OF_LIST := TOP_CF_LIST;
  BOTTOM_OF_LISTâ.C_VAL := CURRENT_STRING;
  IF RELATION_SIZE > 1 THEN
    FOR I:= 2 TO RELATION_SIZE DO
      BEGIN
        CURRENT_STRING := GET_C_VAL (CURRENT_STRING);
        APPEND_STRING (CURRENT_STRING, BOTTOM_OF_LIST)
      END;
  BOTTOM_OF_LISTâ.LINK := NIL
END;


PROCEDURE SET_CISCRETE_BLOCK (IN_REC : ATTR_REC; ATTR_NR : INTEGER;
                             VAR ANSWER : I_POINTER);

(* GENERATES THE CISCRETE BLOCKS OF ATTRIBUTE VALUES TO BE USED. *)

VAR
  R, Q : I_FCINTER;
  I, J, K : INTEGER;
  CONTROL : ARFAY (.1..20.) OF INTEGER;

BEGIN
  FOR I:= 1 TC IN_REC.UPPER_BOUNC DO
    CONTRCL (.I.) := ATTR_NR * IN_REC.REL_PROPORTIONS (.I.) DIV 100;
  NEW (R);
  ANSWER := Râc IN_REC.UPPER_BOUND DO
  FOR I:= 1 TC IN_REC.UPPER_BOUND DO
    BEGIN
      FCR J:= 1 TO CONTROL (.I.) DO
        BEGIN
          Râ.I_VAL := I;
          NEW (Râ.LINK);
          R := Rj
          F := Râ.LINK
        END
    END;
  Qâ.LINK := NIL
END; (* SET_CISCRETE_BLOCK *)
```

```
BEGIN (* GENERATE *)

NAME_OF_FILE:= 'NAME = ' || IN_REC.ATTR_NAME || '.ATTRIBUT';
REWRITEOLTFILE, NAME_CF_FILE);
MARK(B);
CASE IN_REC.GEN_MODE CF
    1:
       BEGIN
          INT_SEQUENTIAL(IN_REC,RELATION_SIZE, IPTR1);
          REPEAT
              WRITELN(CUTFILE, IPTR1@.I_VAL : IN_REC.STRING_LENGTH);
              IPTR1:= IPTR1@.LINK;
          UNTIL IPTR1 = NIL;
       END; (* CASE 1 *)
    2:
       BEGIN
          INTRANDOM(IN_REC,RELATION_SIZE,IPTR1);
          REPEAT
              WRITELN(CUTFILE, IPTR1@.I_VAL : IN_REC.STRING_LENGTH);
              IPTR1:= IPTR1@.LINK
          UNTIL IPTR1= NIL;
       END; (* CASE 2 *)
    3:
       BEGIN
          INT_UNIQUE_RANDOM(IN_REC,RELATION_SIZE,IPTR1);
          REPEAT
              WRITELN(CUTFILE, IPTR1@.I_VAL : IN_REC.STRING_LENGTH);
              IPTR1:= IPTR1@.LINK
          UNTIL IPTR1= NIL;
       END; (* CASE 3 *)
    4:
       BEGIN
          CHAR_SEQ(IN_REC,RELATION_SIZE,CPTR1);
          REPEAT
              WRITELN(CUTFILE, CPTR1@.C_VAL);
              CPTR1:= CPTR1@.LINK
          UNTIL CPTR1 = NIL;
       END; (* CASE 4 *)
    5:
       BEGIN
          INTRANDOM(IN_REC,RELATION_SIZE,IPTR1);
          NAME_CF_FILE:= 'NAME = ' || IN_REC.VALUE_SET_NAME ||
             '.VALUESET';
```

80

```
RESET (STRFILE, NAME_OF_FILE);
REPEAT
  VAL_AR := IPTR1@.I_VAL;
  SEEK(STRFILE;VAL_NR);
  GET(STRFILE);VAL_NR);
  WRITELN(OUTFILE, STRFILE@);
  IPTR1 := IPTR1@.LINK;
UNTIL IPTR1 = NIL;
CLOSE (STRFILE);
END; (* CASE 5 *)

6:
BEGIN
  SET_DISCRETE-BLOCK(IN_REC,RELATION_SIZE,IPTR1);
  NAME_OF_FILE:= 'VALUESET '|| IN_REC.VALUE_SET_NAME ||
  RESET(STRFILE, NAME_OF_FILE);
  REPEAT
    VAL_AR:= IPTR1@.I_VAL;
    SEEK(STRFILE;VAL_NR);
    GET(STRFILE);VAL_NR);
    WRITELN(OUTFILE, STRFILE@);
    IPTR1:= IPTR1@.LINK;
  UNTIL IPTR1 = NIL;
  CLOSE (STRFILE)
END; (* CASE 6 *)

END (* CASE *);
END (* GENERATE *);

PROCEDURE COLLATE (ATTR_INFO : ATTR_ARRAY; ATTR_CREATED : INTEGER);

(* COLLECTS THE ATTRIBUTE VALUES FROM THEIR FILES AND GENERATES TUPLES INTO THE
RELATION FILE. *)

VAR
  I,J,K,L        : INTEGER;
  BUFF_STRING    : STRING (255);
  FILE_ARRAY     : ARRAY (.1..NUMBER_OF_ATTRIBUTES.) OF TEXT;
  DESCRIPTION    : TEXT;
  RELATION_FILE  : FILE OF PACKED ARRAY (.1..LRECL.) OF CHAR;
  NAME_OF_FILE   : STRING (25);
  SPACE_LENGTH   : INTEGER;

BEGIN
  NAME_OF_FILE := 'NAME = ' || RELATION_NAME || '.DESCRIPT';
```

```pascal
REWRITE (DESCRIPTION, NAME_OF_FILE);
WRITELN (DESCRIPTION, RELATION_NAME : 14);
WRITELN (DESCRIPTION, ATTR_CREATED : 9, ' ATTRIBUTES');
WRITELN (DESCRIPTION, RELATION_SIZE : 9, ' TUPLES');
WRITELN (DESCRIPTION, '    ATTR   SRCE  DEST');
WRITELN (DESCRIPTION, '    NAME   TYPE  TYPE');
WRITELN (DESCRIPTION, '    ----   ----  ----');
FOR I:= 1 TO ATTR_CREATED DO
WITH ATTR_INFO (.I.) DO BEGIN
  WRITE (DESCRIPTION, ATTR_NAME : 8, ' C' : 3, STRING_LENGTH : 3,
         ATTR_TYPE (.1.) : 3);
  IF ATTR_INFO (.I.).ATTR_TYPE (.1.) IN (. 'C','' .) THEN
    WRITELN (DESCRIPTION, ATTR_INFO (.I.).STRING_LENGTH : 3)
  ELSE WRITELN (DESCRIPTION, ATTR_TYPE (.2.) : 1);
END;
CLOSE (DESCRIPTION);
NAME_OF_FILE := 'NAME = ' || RELATION_NAME || '.RELATION';
REWRITE (RELATION_FILE, NAME_OF_FILE);
FOR I:= 1 TO ATTR_CREATED DO
BEGIN
  NAME_OF_FILE := 'NAME = ' || ATTR_INFO (.I.).ATTR_NAME ||
                  '.ATTRIBUT';
  RESET (FILE_ARRAY (.I.), NAME_OF_FILE)
END;
FOR I:= 1 TO RELATION_SIZE DO
BEGIN
  L := 1;
  FOR J:= 1 TO ATTR_CREATED DO
  BEGIN
    READLN (FILE_ARRAY (.J.), BUFF_STRING);
    SPACE_LENGTH := ATTR_INFO (.J.).STRING_LENGTH -
                    LENGTH (BUFF_STRING);
    IF SPACE_LENGTH <> 0
      FOR K:= 1 SPACE_LENGTH DO
      BEGIN
        RELATION_FILE@(.L.) := ' ';
        L := L + 1
      END;
    FOR K:= 1 TO LENGTH (BUFF_STRING) DO
    BEGIN
      RELATION_FILE@(.L.) := BUFF_STRING (.K.);
      L := L + 1
    END
  END
  PUT (RELATION_FILE)
END;
END;
```

82

```
      FOR I := 1 TO #ATTR_CREATED DO
         CLOSE (FILE_ARRAY(.I.));
END;

FUNCTION GET_NC : BOOLEAN;

(* GETS A YES OR NO ANSWER. *)

BEGIN
   GOOD_ANSWER := FALSE;
   REPEAT
      READLN (TTYIN, ANSWER);
      IF NOT (ANSWER IN (.'Y','Y','N','N'.)) THEN
         WRITELN (TTYOUT,'INCORRECT INPUT.  ENTER Y OR N ONLY.   TRY AGAIN.')
      ELSE
         BEGIN
            GOOD_ANSWER := TRUE;
            GET_NC := ANSWER IN (.'N','N'.)
         END
   UNTIL GOOD_ANSWER;
   WRITELN (ANSWER)
END;

BEGIN
   TERMIN(TTYIN);
   TERMOUT(TTYOUT);
   GOOD_LETTER := (.'A'..'I','J'..'R','S'..'Z','A'..'I','J'..'R','S'..'Z'.);
   GOOD_LETTER := GOOD_LETTER + (.'0'..'9'.);
   WHILE NOT (DONE_RELATIONS) DO
      BEGIN
         GET_RELATION_NAME (RELATION_NAME);
         GET_RELATION_SIZE (RELATION_SIZE);
         ATTR_CREATED := 0;
         WHILE NOT(DONE_ATTRIBUTES) DO BEGIN
            ATTR_CREATED := ATTR_CREATED + 1;
            WITH ATTR_INFO (.ATTR_CREATED.) DO BEGIN
               GET_ATTRIBUTE_NAME (ATTR_NAME);
               GET_ATTRIBUTE_TYPE (ATTR_TYPE);
               CASE ATTR_TYPE (.1.) OF
                  'C','C':STRING_LENGTH (.STRING_LENGTH);
                  'U','U':STRING_LENGTH := 255;
                  'I','I':BEGIN
                             CASE ATTR_TYPE (.2.) OF
                                '1':  STRING_LENGTH := 4;
                                '2':  STRING_LENGTH := 6;
                                '4':  STRING_LENGTH := 11
```

83

```
            END; (* CASE *)
            GET_RANGE(ATTR_TYPE (.2.), LOWER_BOUND,
                      UPPER_BOUND)

        END
    END; (* CASE *)
    GET_MODE (ATTR_TYPE (.1.), GEN_MODE);
    IF (GEN_MODE < 4) AND NOT (ATTR_TYPE (.1.) IN (.'I','I'.))
    THEN GET_RANGE ('4', LOWER_BOUND, UPPER_BOUND);
    IF (GEN_MODE > 4) THEN
    IF GET_VALUE_SET_DATA (VALUE_SET_NAME, LOWER_BOUND,UPPER_BOUND);
    IF GEN_MODE = 6 THEN
    GET_PROPORTIONS (REL_PROPORTIONS, UPPER_BOUND);
    IF GEN_MODE IN (.2, 3; 5.) THEN
    BEGIN
        WRITELN (TTYOUT);
        WRITELN (TTYOUT, 'ENTER INTEGER TO BE USED AS THE SEED ',
                 'IN THE RANDOM NUMBER GENERATOR.');
        ENTER_INT (SEED)
    END
END; (* WITH ATTR_INFO (.ATTR_CREATED.) DO *)
GENERATE (ATTR_INFO (.ATTR_CREATED.) RELATION_SIZE);
IF ATTR_CREATED < NUMBER_OF_ATTRIBUTES THEN
BEGIN
    WRITELN (TTYOUT, 'IF YOU WISH TO CREATE ANOTHER ATTRIBUTE ',
             'FOR THE RELATION "', RELATION_NAME, '" THEN');
    WRITELN (TTYOUT, 'ENTER Y, OTHERWISE ENTER N.');
    DONE_ATTRIBUTES := GET_NO
END
ELSE
    DONE_ATTRIBUTES := TRUE

END;
COLLATE (ATTR_INFO, ATTR_CREATED)
WRITELN (TTYOUT, 'DO YOU WISH TO ENTER ANOTHER RELATION?  ENTER Y ',
DONE_RELATIONS := GET_NO

END
END.
```

84

APPENDIX C

Database Generator Program (MVS PascalVS)

```
THIS IS THE MVS (BATCH) VERSION OF THE RELATION GENERATOR.

       SEE THE VM/CMS VERSION FOR COMMENTS.

PROGRAM GR122 (INPUT, OUTPUT);

CONST  NUMBER_OF_ATTRIBUTES = 25;
       NAME_LENGTH = 8;
       FILE_NAME_LENGTH = 17;
       STRLEN = 25;
       LRECL = 122;

TYPE   NAME = STRING (8) ;
       ATTRIBUTE_TYPE = PACKED ARRAY (.1..2.) OF CHAR;
       ARRAY_OF_PROPORTIONS = ARRAY (.1..20.) OF INTEGER;
       ATTR_REC = RECORD
          ATTR_NAME : NAME;
          ATTR_TYPE : ATTRIBUTE_TYPE;
          STRING_LENGTH : INTEGER;
          LOWER_BOUND : INTEGER;
          UPPER_BOUND : INTEGER;
          GEN_MODE : INTEGER;
          VALUE_SET_NAME : NAME;
          REL_PROPORTIONS : ARRAY_OF_PROPORTIONS;
          SEET : INTEGER
       END;
       ALPH = SET OF CHAR;
       ATTR_ARRAY = ARRAY (.1..NUMBER_OF_ATTRIBUTES.) OF ATTR_REC;

VAR    DONE_RELATIONS, DONE_ATTRIBUTES, GOOD_ANSWER : BOOLEAN;
       ANSWER : CHAR;
       RELATION_NAME : NAME;
       TEMP_STRING : STRING (20);
       GOOD_LETTER : ALPH;
       I,SIZE,TEST,ATTR_CREATED,VALU ,TYPE_SIZE,RELATION_SIZE,TOTAL : INTEGER;
       ATTR_INFO : ATTR_ARRAY;
       FILE_ARRAY : ARRAY (.1..NUMBER_OF_ATTRIBUTES.) OF TEXT;

PROCEDURE ENTER_INT ( VAR SUM : INTEGER );

VAR TEMP : STRING (80);

BEGIN
   READLN (TEMP);
      IF LENGTH (TEMP) > 15 THEN
         TEMP := SUBSTR (TEMP, 1, 15);
```

85

```
END; READSTR (TEMP, SUM)

PROCEDURE GET_NAME (VAR FILE_NAME : NAME);

BEGIN
  READLN (FILE_NAME)
END;

PROCEDURE GET_RELATION_NAME (VAR RELATION_NAME : NAME);

BEGIN
  GET_NAME (RELATION_NAME)
END;

PROCEDURE GET_RELATION_SIZE (VAR RELATION_SIZE : INTEGER);

BEGIN ENTER_INT (RELATION_SIZE);
END;

PROCEDURE GET_ATTRIBUTE_NAME (VAR ATTR_NAME : NAME);

BEGIN
  GET_NAME (ATTR_NAME)
END;

PROCEDURE GET_ATTRIBUTE_TYPE (VAR ATTR_TYPE : ATTRIBUTE_TYPE);

BEGIN
  ATTR_TYPE (.2.) := ' ';
  READ (ATTR_TYPE (.1.));
  IF NOT EOLN THEN
    READLN (ATTR_TYPE (.2.))
END;

PROCEDURE GET_MODE (FLAG_CHAR : CHAR; VAR GEN_MODE : INTEGER);

BEGIN ENTER_INT (GEN_MODE)
END;

PROCEDURE GET_RANGE (INT_TYPE : CHAR; VAR LOW, HIGH : INTEGER);

BEGIN ENTER_INT (LOW);
```

```
END;  ENTER_INT (HIGH)

PROCEDURE GET_VALUE_SET_DATA (VAR VALUE_SET_NAME : NAME;
                             VAR LOWER_BOUND, UPPER_BOUND : INTEGER);

BEGIN
  GET_NAME (VALUE_SET_NAME);
  ENTER_INT (UPPER_BOUND)
END;

PROCEDURE GET_PROPORTIONS (VAR PROPORTIONS : ARRAY_OF_PROPORTIONS;
                           UPPER_BOUND : INTEGER);

VAR I : INTEGER;

BEGIN
  FOR I := 1 TO UPPER_BOUND DO
    ENTER_INT (PROPORTIONS (.I.))
END;

PROCEDURE GENERATE (IN_REC : ATTR_REC; NUMBER_TO_GENERATE, ATTR_CREATED :
                    INTEGER);

TYPE
  MARKP = @INTEGER;
  I_POINTER = @I_NODE;
  I_NODE = RECORD
    I_VAL : INTEGER;
    LINK : I_POINTER
  END;
  C_POINTER = @C_NODE;
  C_NODE = RECORD
    C_VAL : STRING(STR_LEN);
    LINK : C_POINTER
  END;

VAR
  B        : MARKP;
  IPTR     : I_POINTER;
  CPTR     : C_POINTER;
  VAL_NR   : INTEGER;
  SET_VAL  : STRING(STR_LEN);
  ATTR_NR  : INTEGER;
  OUTFILE  : TEXT;
  NAME_OF_FILE : STRING (25);
  STRFILE  : FILE OF STRING (STR_LEN);
```

87

```
PROCEDURE INT_SEQUENTIAL (IN_REC : ATTR_REC; RELATION_SIZE : INTEGER;
     VAR TOP_OF_LIST : I_POINTER);

VAR
     I : INTEGER;
     CUR_NODE : I_POINTER;

BEGIN
     NEW (TOP_OF_LIST);
     CUR_NODE := TOP_OF_LIST;
     CUR_NODE@.I_VAL := IN_REC.LOWER_BOUND;
     IF RELATION_SIZE > 1 THEN
          FOR I:=IN_REC.LOWER_BOUND+ 1 TO IN_REC.LOWER_BOUND + RELATION_SIZE -1 DO
               BEGIN
                    NEW (CUR_NODE@.LINK);
                    CUR_NODE := CUR_NODE@.LINK;
                    CUR_NODE@.I_VAL := I
               END;
     CUR_NODE@.LINK := NIL
END;

PROCEDURE INTRANDOM (IN_REC : ATTR_REC; ATTR_NR : INTEGER; VAR ANSWER
                                                       : I_POINTER);

VAR
     NUM, I, LOW, HIGH : INTEGER;
     P,Q : I_POINTER;
     RND_NBR, REAL_NUM : REAL;

BEGIN
     LOW := IN_REC.LOWER_BOUND;
     HIGH := IN_REC.UPPER_BOUND;
     RND_NBR := RANDOM (IN_REC.SEED);
     REAL_NUM := (LOW - RND_NBR * LOW) + RND_NBR * HIGH;
     NUM := ROUND (REAL_NUM);
     NEW (P);
     ANSWER := P;
     P@.I_VAL := NUM;
     FOR I:= 2 TO ATTR_NR DO
          BEGIN
               RND_NBR := RANDOM (0);
               REAL_NUM :=(LOW - RND_NBR * LOW) + RND_NBR * HIGH;
               NUM := ROUND (REAL_NUM);
               NEW (Q);
               P@.LINK := Q;
               P := Q;
               P@.I_VAL := NUM;
               IF I = ATTR_NR THEN
```

88

```
              P@.LINK := NIL
END; (* INTRANDCM *)


PROCEDURE INT_UNIQUE_RANDGM (IN_REC : ATTR_REC; ATTR_NR : INTEGER;
                            VAR ANSWER : T_PCINTER);

TYPE
   T_PTR = @T_NODE;
   T_NODE = RECORD
       I_VAL : INTEGER;
       LOW_PTR : T_PTR;
       HIGH_PTR : T_PTR;
   END;

VAR
   BOTTOM, STORAGE_TREE : I_POINTER;
   SEARCH_TREE, NEXT_PTR, LAST_PTR : T_PTR;
   NUM, I, LCW, HIGH : INTEGER;
   RND_NBR, REAL_NUM : REAL;
   LOW_FLAG : BOOLEAN;

FUNCTION UNIQUE (NUM : INTEGER; VAR LOW : BOOLEAN) : BOOLEAN;
   VAR    IS_UNIQUE : BOOLEAN;

BEGIN
   NEXT_PTR := SEARCH_TREE;
   IS_UNIQUE := TRUE;
   WHILE (NEXT_PTR <> NIL) AND IS_UNIQUE DO
       IF NEXT_PTR@.I_VAL = NUM THEN
           IS_UNIQUE := FALSE
       ELSE
           BEGIN
               LAST_PTR := NEXT_PTR;
               IF NEXT_PTR@.I_VAL > NUM THEN
                   BEGIN
                       LOW := TRUE;
                       NEXT_PTR := NEXT_PTR@.LOW_PTR
                   END
               ELSE
                   BEGIN
                       LOW := FALSE;
                       NEXT_PTR := NEXT_PTR@.HIGH_PTR
                   END
           END;
   UNIQUE := IS_UNIQUE
END;
```

89

```
END;

PROCEDURE STORE_SEARCH_TREE (NUM : INTEGER; LOW : BOOLEAN);

BEGIN
   IF LOW THEN
      BEGIN
         NEW(LAST_PTR@.LOW_PTR);
         NEXT_PTR := LAST_PTR@.LOW_PTR
      END
   ELSE
      BEGIN
         NEW(LAST_PTR@.HIGH_PTR);
         NEXT_PTR := LAST_PTR@.HIGH_PTR
      END;
   NEXT_PTR@.I_VAL := NUM;
   NEXT_PTR@.LOW_PTR := NIL;
   NEXT_PTR@.HIGH_PTR := NIL
END;

PROCEDURE STORE_STORAGE_TREE (NUM : INTEGER);

BEGIN
   NEW(BOTTOM@.LINK);
   BOTTOM := BOTTOM@.LINK;
   BOTTOM@.I_VAL := NUM
END;

BEGIN (* INI UNIQUE RANDOM *)
   WRITELN (TIA INTRANDOM);
   LOW := IN_REC.LOWER BOUND;
   HIGH := IN_REC.UPPER BOUND;
   RND_NBR := RANDOM (IN_REC.SEED);
   REAL_NUM := (LOW - LOW * RND_NBR) + HIGH * RND_NBR;
   NUM := RCUNC(REAL_NUM);
   NEW(ANSWER);
   STORAGE_TREE := ANSWER;
   STORAGE_TREE@.I_VAL := NUM;
   BOTTOM := STORAGE_TREE;
   NEW(SEARCH_TREE);
   SEARCH_TREE@.I_VAL := NUM;
   SEARCH_TREE@.LOW_PTR := NIL;
   SEARCH_TREE@.HIGH_PTR := NIL;
   NEXT_PTR := SEARCH_TREE;
   FOR I := 2 10 ATTR_NR DO
      BEGIN
         RND_NER := RANDOM (O);
         REAL_NUM := (LOW - LOW * RND_NBR) + HIGH * RND_NBR;
```

90

```
            NUM := ROUND (REAL_NUM);
            WHILE NOT (UNIQUE (NUM, LOW_FLAG)) DO
                IF NUM = HIGH THEN
                    NUM := LOW
                ELSE
                    NUM := NUM + 1;
            STORE_SEARCH_TREE (NUM, LOW_FLAG);
            STORE_STORAGE_TREE (NUM);
        END;
        BOTTOM.LINK := NIL
    END; (* INT_UNIQUE_RANDOM *)


PROCEDURE CHAR_SEC(IN_REC :ATTR_REC; RELATION_SIZE : INTEGER;
    VAR TOP_OF_LIST : C_POINTER);

    VAR

        LAST_CHAR : CHAR;
        FIRST_CHARS : STRING(STR_LEN);
        I : INTEGER;
        BOTTOM,CF_LIST : C_POINTER;
        CURRENT_STRING : STRING (STR_LEN);

FUNCTION GET_C_VAL (C_VAL : STRING(STR_LEN)) : STRING (STR_LEN);

    VAR LEN : INTEGER;

FUNCTION SUC (A_CHAR : CHAR ) : STRING(STR_LEN);

BEGIN
    REPEAT
        A_CHAR := SLCC (A_CHAR)
    UNTIL A_CHAR IN GOOD_LETTER;
    SUC := STR (A_CHAR)
END;

BEGIN (* GET_C_VAL *)
    LEN := LENGTH (C_VAL);
    IF (* LEN = 0 THEN DO NOTHING ELSE IF *)
        LEN <> 0 THEN
        BEGIN
            LAST_CHAR := C_VAL (.LEN.);
            FIRST_CHARS := SUBSTR (C_VAL, 1, LEN - 1);
            IF LAST_CHAR = 'Z' THEN
                GET_C_VAL := GET_C_VAL (FIRST_CHARS) || STR ('A')
            ELSE GET_C_VAL := FIRST_CHARS || SUC (LAST_CHAR)
```

91

```
END;

PROCEDURE APPEND_STRING (CURRENT_STRING : STRING(STR_LEN); VAR BOTTOM_OF_LIST :
                         C_POINTER);

BEGIN
  NEW(BOTTOM_OF_LIST@.LINK);
  BOTTOM_OF_LIST := BOTTOM_OF_LIST@.LINK;
  BOTTOM_OF_LIST@.C_VAL := CURRENT_STRING
END;

BEGIN (* CHAR SEQ *)
  NEW(TOP_OF_LIST);
  CURRENT_STRING := '';
  FOR I := 1 TO IN_REC.STRING_LENGTH DO
    CURRENT_STRING := CURRENT_STRING || 'A';
  BOTTOM_OF_LIST := TOP_OF_LIST;
  BOTTOM_OF_LIST@.C_VAL := CURRENT_STRING;
  IF RELATION_SIZE > 1 THEN
    FOR I := 2 TO RELATION_SIZE DO
      BEGIN
        CURRENT_STRING := GET_C_VAL (CURRENT_STRING);
        APPEND_STRING (CURRENT_STRING, BOTTOM_OF_LIST)
      END;
  BOTTOM_OF_LIST@.LINK := NIL
END;

PROCEDURE SET_DISCRETE_BLOCK (IN_REC : ATTR_REC; ATTR_NR : INTEGER;
                              VAR ANSWER : I_POINTER);

VAR
  R, Q : I_POINTER;
  I, J, K : INTEGER;
  CONTROL : ARRAY (.1..20.) OF INTEGER;

BEGIN
  FOR I := 1 TO IN_REC.UPPER_BOUND DO
    CONTROL (.I.) := ATTR_NR * IN_REC.REL_PROPORTIONS (.I.) DIV 100;
  NEW (R);
  ANSWER := R;
  FOR I := 1 TO IN_REC.UPPER_BOUND DO
    BEGIN
      FOR J := 1 TO CONTROL (.I.) DO
        BEGIN
          R@.I_VAL := I;
```

```
                NEW (R@.LINK);
        END;        G := R;
 END;(* SET_DISCRETE_BLOCK *)   F := R@.LINK
                             END


BEGIN (* GENERATE *)
    REWRITE(FILE_ARRAY (.ATTR_CREATED.));
    MARK(B);
    CASE IN_REC.GEN_MODE OF
    1:  BEGIN
            INT SEQUENTIAL(IN_REC,RELATION_SIZE, IPTR1);
            REPEAT
                WRITELN(FILE_ARRAY (.ATTR_CREATEC.), IPTR1@.I_VAL :
                        IN_REC.STRING_LENGTH);
                IPTR1 := IPTR1@.LINK;
            UNTIL IPTR1 = NIL;
        END;(* CASE 1 *)

    2:  BEGIN
            INT RANDOM(IN_REC,RELATION_SIZE,IPTR1);
            REPEAT
                WRITELN(FILE_ARRAY (.ATTR_CREATEC.), IPTR1@.I_VAL :
                        IN_REC.STRING_LENGTH);
                IPTR1 := IPTR1@.LINK
            UNTIL IPTR1 = NIL;
        END;(* CASE 2 *)

    3:  BEGIN
            INT UNIQUE_RANDOM(IN_REC,RELATION_SIZE,IPTR1);
            REPEAT
                WRITELN(FILE_ARRAY (.ATTR_CREATEC.), IPTR1@.I_VAL :
                        IN_REC.STRING_LENGTH);
                IPTR1 := IPTR1@.LINK
            UNTIL IPTR1 = NIL;
        END;(* CASE 3 *)

    4:  BEGIN
            CHAR SEQ(IN_REC,RELATION_SIZE,CPTR1);
            REPEAT
```

```
            WRITELN(FILE_ARRAY (.ATTR_CREATED.), CPTR1@.C_VAL);
            CPTR1:= CPTR1@.LINK
      UNTIL CPTR1 = NIL;
   END; (* CASE 4 *)

5: BEGIN
      IN_REC.LOWER_BOUND := 1;
      IN_RANDOM(IN_REC;RELATION_SIZE,IPTR1);
      NAME_OF_FILE := 'DDNAME ='||IN_REC.VALUE_SET_NAME;
      RESET(STRFILE, NAME_OF_FILE);
      REPEAT
         VAL_NR := IPTR1@.I_VAL;
         SEEK(STRFILE;VAL_NR);
         GET(STRFILE);
         WRITELN(FILE_ARRAY (.ATTR_CREATED.), STRFILE@);
         IPTR1:= IPTR1@.LINK;
      UNTIL IPTR1 = NIL;
      CLOSE (STRFILE)
   END; (* CASE 5 *)

6: BEGIN
      SET_DISCRETE_BLOCK(IN_REC,RELATION_SIZE,IPTR1);
      NAME_OF_FILE := 'DDNAME ='||IN_REC.VALUE_SET_NAME;
      RESET(STRFILE, NAME_OF_FILE);
      REPEAT
         VAL_NR:= IPTR1@.I_VAL;
         SEEK(STRFILE;VAL_NR);
         GET(STRFILE);
         WRITELN(FILE_ARRAY (.ATTR_CREATED.), STRFILE@);
         IPTR1:= IPTR1@.LINK;
      UNTIL IPTR1 = NIL;
      CLOSE (STRFILE)
   END; (* CASE 6 *)

   END (* CASE *);
   CLOSE (FILE_ARRAY (.ATTR_CREATED.));
END RELEASE(B) (* GENERATE *);

PROCEDURE COLLATE (ATTR_INFO : ATTR_ARRAY; ATTR_CREATED : INTEGER);

VAR
   I,J,K,L      : INTEGER;
   BUFF_STRING  : STRING (STR_LEN);
   DESCRIPTION  : TEXT;
```

94

```
            RELATION_FILE : FILE OF PACKED ARRAY (.1..LRECL.) OF CHAR;
            NAME_OF_FILE : STRING (25);
            SPACE_LENGTH : INTEGER;

BEGIN
      REWRITE (RELATION_FILE);
      FOR RESET (FILE_ARRAY.CREATED DO
      FOR RESET (FILE_ARRAY (.I.));
      FOR I := 1 TO RELATION_SIZE DO
         BEGIN
            IF I MOD 100 = 0 THEN WRITELN (I);
            L := 1;
            FOR J := 1 TO ATTR_CREATED DO
            BEGIN
               READLN (FILE_ARRAY (.J.), BUFF_STRING);
               IF ATTR_INFO (.J..ATTR.TYPE (.J.) = ' I ';' I ';' .) THEN
               FOR J := 1 TO ATTR_INFO (.J..STRING_LENGTH DO
                  IF BUFF_STRING (.K.) = ' ' THEN
                     BUFF_STRING (.K.) := '0';

               WHILE BUFF_STRING (.1.) = ' ' DO
                  BUFF_STRING := SUBSTR (BUFF_STRING, 2, LENGTH
                     (BUFF_STRING) - 1 );
               FOR K := 1 TO ATTR_INFO (.J.).STRING_LENGTH DO
                  BEGIN
                     RELATION_FILE@ (.L.) := BUFF_STRING (.K.);
                     L := L + 1
                  END

            END;
            RELATION_FILE@ (.LRECL.) := 'X';
            PUT (RELATION_FILE);
         END;
      FOR I := 1 TO ATTR_CREATED DO
         CLOSE (FILE_ARRAY (.I.));
      CLOSE (RELATION_FILE)
END;

FUNCTION GET_NO : BOOLEAN;

BEGIN  READLN (ANSWER);
       GET_NO := ANSWER IN (.'N','N'.)

END;

BEGIN
GOOD_LETTER:=(.'A'..'I','J'..'R','S'..'Z','A'..'I','J'..'R','S'..'Z'.);
       RESET (INPUT);
       REWRITE (OUTPUT);
```

95

```
WHILE NOT (DCNE_RELATICNS) DO
  BEGIN
    GET RELATION_NAME (RELATION_NAME);
    WRITELN (RELATICN_NAME);
    GET RELATION_SIZE (RELATION_SIZE);
    ATTR_CREATED := 0;
    WHILE NOT(DCNE_ATTRIBUTES) CO BEGIN
      ATTR_CREATED := ATTR_CREATED + 1;
      WITH ATTR_INFO (.ATTR_CREATED.) DO BEGIN
        GET ATTRIBUTE_NAME (ATTR_NAME);
        WRITELN(ATTR_NAME);
        GET ATTRIBUTE_TYPE (ATTR_TYPE);
        CASE ATTR_TYPE(.1.) CF
          'C','C':READLN (STRING_LENGTH);
          'U','U':STRING_LENGTH := 255;
          'I','I':BEGIN
            CASE ATTR TYPE (.2.) OF
              '1': STRING_LENGTH := 4;
              '2': STRING_LENGTH := 6;
              '4': STRING_LENGTH := 11
            END; (* CASE #*)
            GET_RANGE(ATTR_TYPE (.2.), LOWER_BOUND,
                      UPPER_BOUND)
          END
        END; (* CASE *)
        GET_MODE (ATTR_TYPE (.1.), GEN_MODE);
        IF (GEN_MODE (ATTR_TYPE < 4) AND NOT (ATTR_TYPE (.1.) IN (.'I',' '.))
          THEN GET RANGE ('4', LOWER_BOUND, UPPER_BOUND);
        IF (GEN_MODE > 4) THEN
          GET_VALUE_SET DATA (VALUE_SET_NAME, LOWER_BOUND,UPPER_BOUND);
        IF GET_MODE = 6 THEN
          GET_PROPORTIONS (REL_PRCPORTIONS, UPPER_BOUND);
        IF GEN_MODE IN (.2, 3, 5.) THEN
          ENTER_INT (.SEED.)
      END; (* WITH ATTR_INFO (.ATTR_CREATED.) DO *)
      GENERATE (ATTR_INFO (.ATTR_CREATED.), RELATION_SIZE, ATTR_CREATED);
      IF ATTR CREATED < NUMBER_OF_ATTRIBUTES THEN
        DONE_ATTRIBUTES := GET_NO
      ELSE
        DONE_ATTRIBUTES := TRUE
    END;
    COLLATE (ATTR_INFO, ATTR_CREATED)
    DCNE_RELATIONS := GET_NO
  END
END.
//GO.RELATION DD LNIT=3330V,MSVGP=PUB4A,DISP=(NEW,CATLG,DELETE),
//  SPACE=(CYL,(4,4),RLSE),
//  DCB=(RECFM=FB,LRECL=122,BLKSIZE=12932),DSNAME=MSS.S2112.TO1L100
```

```
//GO.COLORS   CD DISP=SHR,DSNAME=MSS.S2I12.VALUESET.TWO
//GO.LETTERS  CD DISP=SHR,DSNAME=MSS.S2I12.VALUESET.THREE
//PASCAL01 DD UNIT=SYSDA,DISP=(NEW,DELETE),
// SPACE=(CYL,(1,1),RLSE),DCB=(RECFM=FB,LRECL=27,BLKSIZE=1350),
// DSN=&&P201
//GO.PASCAL02 DD UNIT=SYSDA,DISP=(NEW,DELETE),
// SPACE=(CYL,(1,1),RLSE),DCB=(RECFM=FB,LRECL=27,BLKSIZE=1350),
// DSN=&&P202
//GO.PASCAL03 DD UNIT=SYSDA,DISP=(NEW,DELETE),
// SPACE=(CYL,(1,1),RLSE),DCB=(RECFM=FB,LRECL=27,BLKSIZE=1350),
// DSN=&&P203
//GO.PASCAL04 DD UNIT=SYSDA,DISP=(NEW,DELETE),
// SPACE=(CYL,(1,1),RLSE),DCB=(RECFM=FB,LRECL=27,BLKSIZE=1350),
// DSN=&&P204
//GO.PASCAL05 CD UNIT=SYSDA,DISP=(NEW,DELETE),
// SPACE=(CYL,(1,1),RLSE),DCB=(RECFM=FB,LRECL=27,BLKSIZE=1350),
// DSN=&&P205
//GO.PASCAL06 GD UNIT=SYSDA,DISP=(NEW,DELETE),
// SPACE=(CYL,(1,1),RLSE),DCB=(RECFM=FB,LRECL=27,BLKSIZE=1350),
// DSN=&&P206
//GO.PASCAL07 DD UNIT=SYSDA,DISP=(NEW,DELETE),
// SPACE=(CYL,(1,1),RLSE),DCB=(RECFM=FB,LRECL=27,BLKSIZE=1350),
// DSN=&&P207
//GO.PASCAL08 DD UNIT=SYSDA,DISP=(NEW,DELETE),
// SPACE=(CYL,(1,1),RLSE),DCB=(RECFM=FB,LRECL=27,BLKSIZE=1350),
// DSN=&&P208
//GO.PASCAL09 DC UNIT=SYSDA,DISP=(NEW,DELETE),
// SPACE=(CYL,(1,1),RLSE),DCB=(RECFM=FB,LRECL=27,BLKSIZE=1350),
// DSN=&&P209
//GO.PASCAL10 DD UNIT=SYSDA,DISP=(NEW,DELETE),
// SPACE=(CYL,(1,1),RLSE),DCB=(RECFM=FB,LRECL=27,BLKSIZE=1350),
// DSN=&&P210
//GO.PASCAL11 CC UNIT=SYSDA,DISP=(NEW,DELETE),
// SPACE=(CYL,(1,1),RLSE),DCB=(RECFM=FB,LRECL=27,BLKSIZE=1350),
// DSN=&&P211
//GO.PASCAL12 CC UNIT=SYSCA,DISP=(NEW,DELETE),
// SPACE=(CYL,(1,1),RLSE),DCB=(RECFM=FB,LRECL=27,BLKSIZE=1350),
// DSN=&&P212
//GO.PASCAL13 CC UNIT=SYSDA,DISP=(NEW,DELETE),
// SPACE=(CYL,(1,1),RLSE),DCB=(RECFM=FB,LRECL=27,BLKSIZE=1350),
// DSN=&&P213
//GO.PASCAL14 CC UNIT=SYSCA,DISP=(NEW,DELETE),
// SPACE=(CYL,(1,1),RLSE),DCB=(RECFM=FB,LRECL=27,BLKSIZE=1350),
// DSN=&&P214
//GO.PASCAL15 DD UNIT=SYSDA,DISP=(NEW,DELETE),
// SPACE=(CYL,(1,1),RLSE),DCB=(RECFM=FB,LRECL=27,BLKSIZE=1350),
// DSN=&&P215
//GO.PASCAL16 GD UNIT=SYSDA,DISP=(NEW,DELETE),
```

97

```
//         SPACE=(CYL,(1,1),RLSE),DCB=(RECFM=FB,LRECL=27,BLKSIZE=1350),
//         DSN=&&P216
//GO.PASCAL17 DD UNIT=SYSDA,DISP=(NEW,DELETE),
//         SPACE=(CYL,(1,1),RLSE),DCB=(RECFM=FB,LRECL=27,BLKSIZE=1350),
//         DSN=&&P217
//GO.PASCAL18 DD UNIT=SYSDA,DISP=(NEW,DELETE),
//         SPACE=(CYL,(1,1),RLSE),DCB=(RECFM=FB,LRECL=27,BLKSIZE=1350),
//         DSN=&&P218
//GO.PASCAL19 DD UNIT=SYSCA,DISP=(NEW,DELETE),
//         SPACE=(CYL,(1,1),RLSE),DCB=(RECFM=FB,LRECL=27,BLKSIZE=1350),
//         DSN=&&P219
//GO.PASCAL20 DD UNIT=SYSCA,CISP=(NEW,DELETE),
//         SPACE=(CYL,(1,1),RLSE),DCB=(RECFM=FB,LRECL=27,BLKSIZE=1350),
//         DSN=&&P220
//GO.PASCAL21 DD UNIT=SYSDA,DISP=(NEW,DELETE),
//         SPACE=(CYL,(1,1),RLSE),DCB=(RECFM=FB,LRECL=27,BLKSIZE=1350),
//         DSN=&&P221
//GO.PASCAL22 DD UNIT=SYSDA,DISP=(NEW,DELETE),
//         SPACE=(CYL,(1,1),RLSE),DCB=(RECFM=FB,LRECL=27,BLKSIZE=1350),
//         DSN=&&P222
//GO.PASCAL23 DD UNIT=SYSDA,DISP=(NEW,DELETE),
//         SPACE=(CYL,(1,1),RLSE),DCB=(RECFM=FB,LRECL=27,BLKSIZE=1350),
//         DSN=&&P223
//GO.PASCAL24 DD UNIT=SYSDA,DISP=(NEW,DELETE),
//         SPACE=(CYL,(1,1),RLSE),DCB=(RECFM=FB,LRECL=27,BLKSIZE=1350),
//         DSN=&&P224
//GO.PASCAL25 DD UNIT=SYSDA,DISP=(NEW,DELETE),
//         SPACE=(CYL,(1,1),RLSE),DCB=(RECFM=FB,LRECL=27,BLKSIZE=1350),
//         DSN=&&P225
//GO.INPUT DD *
IOILIOO
10000
KEY
I4
0
2140C00000
1
MIRRCR
C
11
1
0
2140C00000
Y
RAND
I4
0
```

2140C00000
22
2Y
INIQRAND
I4
0
2140000000
3m
3Y
CHARS
C4
4Y
LETTER
C1
5
LETTERS
26
26Y
PFIVE
C9
6
COLORS
20

99

```
5
5
YPTEN
C
9
6
COLORS
100
100
1000
1000
100
100
10
Y
PTWENTY
C
9
6
COLORS
50
20
200
200
20
Y
PTWENFIV
C
9
6
COLORS
4
25
25
25
YPTHIRFIV
C
9
6
COLORS
```

35
35
30
Y
PFIFTY
C
9
6
COLORS
2
50
50
Y
PSEVENFIV
C
9
6
COLORS
2
75
25
Y
PEIGHTY
C
9
6
COLORS
2
80
20
NN

```
THIS IS THE MVS (BATCH) VERSION OF THE VALUE-SET GENERATOR.
        SEE THE VM/CMS VERSION FOR COMMENTS.

//VCOLORS JOB (2112,0201),'VCOLORS',CLASS=A
//EXEC PASCCG,PARM='VAR(1,80)'
//PASC.SYSIN DD *
PROGRAM MS;

CONST
   STR_LEN = 25;

TYPE
   ELEMENT_POINTER = @E_NODE;
   E_NODE = RECORD
            ELEMENT : STRING (STR_LEN);
            LINK : ELEMENT_POINTER
            END;
   FILE_NAME_TYPE = STRING (8);

VAR
   LIST_POINTER : ELEMENT_POINTER;
   NUMBER       : INTEGER;
   FILE_NAME    : FILE_NAME_TYPE;

PROCEDURE GET_NUMBER (VAR NUMBER : INTEGER);

   VAR
      ANSWER  : STRING (80);

   BEGIN
   READLN (INPUT, ANSWER);
   READSTR (ANSWER, NUMBER)
   END (* GET_NUMBER *);

PROCEDURE GET_SET (NUMBER : INTEGER; VAR LIST_POINTER : ELEMENT_POINTER);

   VAR
      CURRENT_POINTER : ELEMENT_POINTER;
      I, LEN          : INTEGER;
      ELEMENT         : STRING (STR_LEN);

PROCEDURE GET_ELEMENT (ELEMENT_NUMBER : INTEGER; VAR ELEMENT :
      STRING (STR_LEN));
```

102

```
        VAR
          I        : INTEGER;

        BEGIN
          ELEMENT := '';
          FOR I:= 1 TO STR_LEN DO   . . . ;
            READLN (INPUT, ELEMENT);
          WRITELN (ELEMENT, ' IN');
        END (* GET_ELEMENT *);

        BEGIN
          NEW (LIST_POINTER);
          CURRENT_POINTER := LIST_POINTER;
          GET_ELEMENT (I; ELEMENT);
          CURRENT_POINTER@.ELEMENT := ELEMENT;
          IF NUMBER > 1 THEN
            FOR I:= 2 TO NUMBER DO
              BEGIN
                NEW (CURRENT_POINTER@.LINK);
                CURRENT_POINTER := CURRENT_POINTER@.LINK;
                GET_ELEMENT (I, ELEMENT);
                CURRENT_POINTER@.ELEMENT := ELEMENT;
              END;
          CURRENT_POINTER@.LINK := NIL
        END (* GET_SET *);

PROCEDURE WRITE_SET (NUMBER : INTEGER; NAME : FILE_NAME_TYPE;
           LIST_POINTER : ELEMENT_POINTER);

        VAR
          I : INTEGER;
          FILE_STRING : STRING (24);
          SET_FILE : FILE OF STRING (STR_LEN);

        BEGIN
          FILE_STRING := 'DDNAME=' || NAME;
          REWRITE (SET_FILE, FILE_STRING);
          FOR I:= 1 TO NUMBER DO
            BEGIN
              SET_FILE@ := LIST_POINTER@.ELEMENT;
              WRITELN (SET_FILE@);
              PUT (SET_FILE);
              LIST_POINTER := LIST_POINTER@.LINK
            END;
          CLOSE (SET_FILE);
          (* WRITE_SET *)
```

```
FUNCTION NO_MORE : BOOLEAN;

    VAR  ANSWER : STRING (80);

BEGIN
    READLN (INPUT, ANSWER);
    NO_MORE := r ((ANSWER = 'Y') OR (ANSWER = ' '))
END (* NO_MORE *);


BEGIN
    RESET (INPUT);
    REPEAT
        READLN (INPUT, FILE_NAME);
        GET_NUMBER (NUMBER);
        GET_SET (NUMBER, LIST_POINTER);
        WRITE_SET (NUMBER, FILE_NAME, LIST_POINTER)
    UNTIL NO_MORE;
END (* MAKE-SET *);
//GO.COLORS DD UNIT=3330V,MSVGP=PUB4A,DISP=(NEW,CATLG,DELETE),
//      SPACE=(CYL,(4,4),RLSE),
//      DCB=(RECFM=FB,RECL=27,BLKSIZE=27),DSNAME=#SS.S2112.COLORS
//GO.INPUT DC *
COLORS
20
RED
GREEN
BROWN
BLUE
YELLOW
PURPLE
BLACK
WHITE
GOLD
SILVER
PINK
GRAY
SCARLET
TAN
ORANGE
TURQUOISE
MAGENTA
TEAL
VIOLET
ROSE
```

Valueset Generator Program (CMS PASCALVS)

```
(* THIS IS THE VM/CMS VERSION OF THE VALUE SET GENERATOR (VG). BASED ON
   INPUT IT CREATES A FILE FOR USE BY THE RELATION GENERATOR. *)

PROGRAM MS;

CONST
  STR_LEN = 25;

TYPE
  ELEMENT_POINTER = @E_NODE;
  E_NODE = RECORD
    ELEMENT : STRING (STR_LEN);
    LINK : ELEMENT_POINTER
  END;

  FILE_NAME_TYPE = STRING (8);

VAR
  LIST POINTER : ELEMENT_POINTER;
  TTYIN; TTYOUT : TEXT;
  NUMBER : INTEGER;
  FILE_NAME : FILE_NAME_TYPE;

PROCEDURE HELLO;

  WRITELN (TTYOUT);
  WRITELN (TTYOUT);              THIS PROGRAM GENERATES A FILE CONTAINING A VALUE SET.',
  WRITELN (TTYOUT,' ASKED THE'; NAME OF THE FILE IN WHICH YOU WISH TO STORE THE VALUE ',
  WRITELN (TTYOUT,' SET AND THE NUMBER OF EN ');
        'ENTER THE VALUES IN THE VALUE SET. THEN YOU WILL BE ASKED TO ',
  WRITELN (TTYOUT,' VALUES ONE-BY-ONE.');
        'AFTER WHICH YOU WILL BE NOTIFIED THAT THE FILE ',
  WRITELN (TTYOUT,'HAS BEEN SAVED YOU MAY ENTER.');
        'ADDITIONAL VALUE SETS BEFORE TERMINATING THE ',
  WRITELN (TTYOUT,'PROGRAM IF YOU DESIRE THE PRO .');
        'GRAM CURRENTLY STORES VALUE SET ELEMENTS AS 25 ',
  WRITELN (TTYOUT,'CHARACTER LONG STRINGS.');
  WRITELN (TTYOUT);
  WRITELN (TTYOUT);              PRESS THE RETURN KEY TO CONTINUE.');
  READLN (TTYIN);
  WRITELN (TTYOUT);
  ;

PROCEDURE GET_NAME (VAR FILE_NAME : FILE_NAME_TYPE);

(* PROMPTS THE USER FOR A FILE NAME. *)
```

105

```
    VAR
        ANSWER : STRING (80);

BEGIN
    WRITELN (TTYOUT);
    WRITELN (TTYOUT,'WHAT IS THE FILE NAME TO BE USED (8 CHARACTERS ',
             'MAXIMUM) ?');
    READLN (TTYIN, ANSWER);
    IF LENGTH (ANSWER) > 8 THEN
        ANSWER := SUBSTR (ANSWER, 1, 8);
    FILE_NAME := ANSWER
END (* GET_NAME *);

PROCEDURE GET_NUMBER (VAR NUMBER : INTEGER);

(* PROMPTS THE USER FOR THE NUMBER OF VALUES IN THE SET. *)

    VAR
        ANSWER   : STRING (80);

BEGIN
    WRITELN (TTYOUT);
    WRITELN (TTYOUT,'HOW MANY ELEMENTS ARE THERE IN THE SET?');
    READLN (TTYIN, ANSWER);
    READSTR (ANSWER, NUMBER)
END (* GET_NUMBER *);

PROCEDURE GET_SET (NUMBER : INTEGER; VAR LIST_POINTER : ELEMENT_POINTER);

(* PROMPTS THE USER TO ENTER THE SET. *)

    VAR
        CURRENT_POINTER  : ELEMENT_POINTER;
        I, LEN           : INTEGER;
        ELEMENT          : STRING (STR_LEN);

PROCEDURE GET_ELEMENT (ELEMENT_NUMBER : INTEGER; VAR ELEMENT :
                       STRING (STR_LEN));

(* PROMPTS THE USER TO ENTER AN ELEMENT OF THE SET. *)

    VAR
        I    : INTEGER;

BEGIN
```

```pascal
      ELEMENT := '';
      FOR I := 1 TO STR_LEN DO
         ELEMENT := ELEMENT || ' ';
      WRITELN (TTYOUT, 'ENTER ELEMENT #', ELEMENT_NUMBER:4, ' ');
      READLN (TTYIN, ELEMENT)
   END (* GET_ELEMENT *);

BEGIN
   NEW (LIST_POINTER);
   CURRENT_POINTER := LIST_POINTER;
   GET_ELEMENT (1, ELEMENT);
   CURRENT_POINTER@.ELEMENT := ELEMENT;
   IF NUMBER > 1 THEN
      FOR I := 2 TO NUMBER DO
         BEGIN
            NEW (CURRENT_POINTER@.LINK);
            CURRENT_POINTER := CURRENT_POINTER@.LINK;
            GET_ELEMENT (I, ELEMENT);
            CURRENT_POINTER@.ELEMENT := ELEMENT;
         END;
   CURRENT_POINTER@.LINK := NIL
END (* GET_SET *);


PROCEDURE WRITE_SET (NUMBER : INTEGER; NAME : FILE_NAME_TYPE;
                     LIST_POINTER : ELEMENT_POINTER);

(* WRITES THE SET TO A FILE. *)

   VAR
      I : INTEGER;
      FILE_STRING : STRING (24);
      SET_FILE : FILE OF STRING (STR_LEN);

BEGIN
   FILE_STRING := 'NAME = ' || NAME || '.VALLESET';
   REWRITE (SET_FILE, FILE_STRING);
   FOR I := 1 TO NUMBER DO
      BEGIN
         SET_FILE@ := LIST_POINTER@.ELEMENT;
         PUT (SET_FILE);
         LIST_POINTER := LIST_POINTER@.LINK
      END;
   CLOSE (SET_FILE);
   WRITELN (TTYOUT);
   WRITELN (TTYOUT, 'FILE ', NAME:LENGTH (NAME), ' HAS JUST BEEN SAVED.');
END (* WRITE_SET *);
```

107

```pascal
FUNCTION NO_MORE : BOOLEAN;

(* PROMPTS THE USER TO SEE IF HE WANTS TO GENERATE ANOTHER VALUE SET. *)

VAR
    ANSWER : STRING (80);

BEGIN
    WRITELN (TTYOUT);
    WRITELN (TTYOUT,' DO NEED TO GENERATE MORE SETS (Y OR N)? ');
    READLN (TTYIN, ANSWER);
    NO_MORE := ¬ ((ANSWER = 'Y') OR (ANSWER = ' '))
END (* NO_MORE *);

BEGIN
    TERMIN (TTYIN);
    TERMOUT (TTYOUT);
    HELLO;
    REPEAT
        GET_NAME (FILE_NAME);
        IF LENGTH (FILE_NAME) > 0 THEN
            BEGIN
                GET_NUMBER (NUMBER);
                IF NUMBER > 0 THEN
                    BEGIN
                        GET_SET (NUMBER, LIST_POINTER);
                        WRITE_SET (NUMBER, FILE_NAME, LIST_POINTER)
                    END (* LENGTH *);
    UNTIL NO_MORE;
END (* MAKE_SET *).
```

List Of References

1. RQL Handouts, Amperif Corporation, Chatsworth, California.

2. Britton Lee, IDM Software Reference Manual V 1.3, September, 1981.

3. Ryder, C. J., Benchmarking Relational Database Machines' Capabilities in Supporting the Database Administrator's Functions and Responsibilities, M.S. Thesis, Naval Post graduate School, 1983.

4. Bogdanowicz, R. A., Benchmarking the Selection and Projection Operations and Ordering Capabilities of a Relational Database Machine, M.S. Thesis , Naval Postgraduate School, 1983.

5. Crocker, M. D., Benchmarking the Join Operation on a Relational Database Machine, M.S.Thesis , Naval Postgraduate School, 1983.

Bibliography

IBM, Pascal/VS Language Guide, April, 1981.

IBM, Pascal/VS Programming Guide, April, 1981.

Naval Postgraduate School Technical Momorandum, Using
  Pascal/VS at NPS, Joanne Bogart, March, 1982.

Naval Postgraduate School Technical Note No. MVS-01, User's
    Guide to MVS at NPS, W. R. Church Computer Center,
    October, 1982.

Naval Postgraduate School Technical Report No. VM-01,
    User's Guide to VM/CMS at NPS, W. R. Church Computer
    Center, March, 1982.

INITIAL DISTRIBUTION LIST

13. Commander   1
    Naval Security Group Command
    ATTN: CDR T. M. Pigoski, USN (Code G30D)
    3801 Nebraska Avenue, N.W.
    Washington, DC 20390

14. LT Linda Widmaier, USN   1
    3016 Bromley Court
    Woodbridge, VA 22192

15. Curricular Officer, Code 37   1
    Computer Technology
    Naval Postgraduate School
    Monterey, CA 93940